ALWAYS CONNECTED

Also by
SUZANNE GIESEMANN

*The Awakened Way**

Conquer Your Cravings

Droplets of God

In the Silence

It's Your Boat Too

Living a Dream

Love Beyond Words

*Making the Afterlife Connection**

Mediumship

Messages of Hope

*The Priest and the Medium**

The Real Alzheimer's

Still Right Here

Wolf's Message

*Available from Hay House

Please visit:

Hay House USA: www.hayhouse.com®
Hay House Australia: www.hayhouse.com.au
Hay House UK: www.hayhouse.co.uk
Hay House India: www.hayhouse.co.in

ALWAYS CONNECTED

HOW TO FIND COMFORT, CLARITY, AND DIRECTION FROM THE SPIRIT WITHIN

SUZANNE GIESEMANN

HAY HOUSE LLC
Carlsbad, California • New York City
London • Sydney • New Delhi

Published in the United States by: Hay House LLC, www.hayhouse.com®
P.O. Box 5100, Carlsbad, CA, 92018-5100

Cover design: Julie Davison • *Interior design:* Bryn Starr Best

Tradepaper ISBN: 979-8-3186-0134-7
E-book ISBN: 979-8-3186-0135-4
Audiobook ISBN: 979-8-3186-0136-1

1st Printing

Printed in the United States of America

This product uses responsibly sourced papers, including recycled materials and materials from other controlled sources.

The authorized representative in the EU for product safety and compliance is Penguin Random House Ireland, Morrison Chambers, 32 Nassau Street, Dublin D02 YH68, Ireland. https://eu-contact.penguin.ie

Spirit of great healer,
awaken from within this heart.
Peace and Tranquility flow like water.
The time has come to allow
the Light of Nature to free my soul.

— Michael "Wolf" Pasakarnis

CONTENTS

Preface: Hey, Spirit! ix

PART I — Finding Your Connection

Chapter 1: Annihilated. 3

Chapter 2: Aah 17

Chapter 3: Resistance 31

Chapter 4: Snags and Signs 47

Chapter 5: Who's Driving? 61

Chapter 6: Round and Round 75

Chapter 7: Best-Laid Plans 89

Chapter 8: What Is Real?. 99

PART II — Insights from Within

Introduction to Part II 119

Understanding and Embracing Forgiveness . . .129

Hope in Times of Despair. .133

Giving and Receiving Love and Compassion. . .135

Cultivating Patience 138

Managing Anger Constructively. 140

Comfort and Healing After Loss. 143

Discovering Life's Purpose. 146

Practicing Gratitude 149

The Illusion of Perfection 151

Managing Disappointment 153

Inner Peace 155

Strength in Adversity 158
Judgment Versus Discernment 161
Community and Fellowship. 163
Overcoming Temptation 165
Eternal Life 168
Solitude and Reflection 171
Service and Philanthropy. 174
Marriage and Relationships 176
Guides and Angels 179
Dealing with Change. 181
Dealing with Regret. 183
Balancing Humility and Confidence 185
Self-Worth and Acceptance 187
The Power of Surrender 189

Afterword: Now You're Listening 193
Acknowledgments 197
About the Author 199

PREFACE

Hey, Spirit!

You know those memes that try to make you feel old by showing you how much has changed since you were a kid? Some of them are truly funny, like the one I saw recently. It displayed two photos side by side, with the one on the left showing a grocery shelf with 50 varieties of purified water. That side was labeled "Today." The photo on the right was labeled "Back Then" and showed a kid drinking out of a garden hose.

That was me!

No one can argue with the fact that our world has changed a lot, especially in the last decade, thanks in no small part to technology. Social media—once thought to be a positive way to connect with friends and family members—can help bring us together, but it can also be very divisive. We hear far too many stories of feuds fueled by written comments that most people would never say to someone face-to-face.

In my role as a spiritual teacher, I'm known for being fairly grounded, so allow me to say this with a bit of earthy humor: Our challenges today are based on our individual BS . . . our clashing *belief systems*! Without awareness, our worldviews can keep us locked into patterns of thinking, feeling, and acting that don't leave much room for hearing, appreciating, and honoring what each of us is saying.

Many find themselves stuck in cycles of "me against you" and "us against them," endlessly spinning in place without coming together with those around them. It's easy to place blame, but few pause long enough to notice that every time we point a finger at someone else, three fingers are pointing back at ourselves.

I spend a lot of time contemplating such things these days, which might make you think I have a background in philosophy, psychology, or anthropology. Quite the opposite: I have a master's degree in national security affairs, which I earned while on active duty in the U.S. Navy. I served for 20 years and retired with the rank of commander.

My service culminated in the chairman of the Joint Chiefs of Staff asking me to be his aide-de-camp. I worked directly for the head of the U.S. armed forces for a year. It was an exciting assignment that included flying on *Air Force One* with the president and traveling around the world meeting members of congress, kings, queens, and other world leaders.

With this background, you might think I was a bit left-brained, and you would be right. I still am, to a lesser degree, but instead of seeing things strictly in black and white, today my perspective is more flexible. In a change from what I did most of my life, I now view the world through my heart as much as with my physical eyes.

The death of my stepdaughter Susan, a sergeant in the U.S. Marine Corps, was the catalyst for these changes. Susan volunteered to serve in Iraq at the height of U.S. involvement in that country, but her husband felt it was too dangerous for her to deploy there.

Newly married, she listened to him and remained at her assigned duty station in Cherry Point, North Carolina. On June 8, 2006, while crossing the tarmac toward the hangar where she worked on search and rescue helicopters, she was struck to the ground by a bolt of lightning from a storm more than 10 miles away.

The Marines who witnessed the strike rushed to her side and began CPR immediately. When the ambulance arrived, paramedics took over. They continued chest compressions until doctors at the nearest trauma unit assumed her care. The medical team did all they could for seven hours, but they couldn't save Susan or her unborn baby, Liam Tyler, my husband's and my only grandchild.

I was no stranger to tragedy, having personally witnessed the carnage of the terrorist attacks on 9/11. On that day, I was flying with the chairman to Europe, where my boss was to be knighted by Queen Elizabeth. Upon hearing the news from New York and Washington, DC, we turned around over the Atlantic.

Our flight path took us directly over Manhattan. By that time, all other planes had been grounded, leaving us aboard the last aircraft in U.S. airspace. I looked out the small windows at the smoke billowing up from the World Trade Center as we continued to Washington. Back at our battered office building, the Pentagon, I stared at the gaping hole where colleagues in uniforms just like mine had sat at their desks only hours earlier.

I wrestled then and in the weeks that followed to understand the nature of good and evil and why some people die far short of what we consider a full lifetime. My lack of religious upbringing and ignorance about spiritual topics left me few tools to deal with death. I had only a vague sense that there is more to life than meets the eye.

I found no satisfactory answers to the deep questions that 9/11 engendered. My parents had conditioned me to only express positive feelings, so I buried the deep grief and angst I was feeling. Five years later, Susan's passing brought those emotions to the surface. I held everything inside as best I could until the night before her funeral. Lying in the darkness of the visiting officers' quarters, my body began to quake.

Afraid that I might cry and add to the pain my husband, Ty, was suffering, I leapt from the bed, threw on street clothes, and told him I had to go for a walk. Normally he wouldn't let me go outside alone at three o'clock in the morning, but this time—lost in his own grief—he didn't stop me. I grabbed the keys to our rental car on my way out the door and rushed across the dark parking lot. Something inside me must have known I needed a place where I wouldn't be heard, for I climbed into the car and let out a long, guttural howl.

This set off a chain reaction that surely met the definition of a meltdown. I pounded the steering wheel and stamped on the floorboards as I wailed and cursed at a God I didn't know. Only recently did my sister-in-law Lynn remind me that after my breakdown, I knocked on the door of her room, which was down the hall from ours. I had completely suppressed all memories of having done so.

I now recall telling her that I didn't know what to do or how to handle what I was feeling. I know she was dealing with her own pain, having loved Susan deeply, but Lynn listened and put her arms around me as I sobbed. She helped me calm down enough to return to bed without further upsetting Ty.

I realize now what I didn't understand then: The God we naturally turn to in times of trouble did hear my cries and guided me to exactly who and what I needed in that moment. The formless source of all that is doesn't have a body. Instead, this infinitely intelligent and loving creator appeared in that moment embodied as my sister-in-law, Lynn.

We need not be aware that the one indivisible spirit breathes and lives as us. Such insights arise by grace in moments of crisis, deep connection, or sudden clarity. Both despair and immense beauty can have the same effect. For me the recognition that there is a vitalizing power within each of us that cannot be extinguished and to which we are always connected became an undeniable certainty at the viewing, when I gazed at Susan's lifeless body.

I suddenly knew why we call our deepest essence "light." It is something that can't be captured and kept in a jar like a firefly. It sparkles and dances and shows its true nature in people like Susan, whose shining presence draws us to them like a moth to a flame. It may go out within the body at the time of physical death, but ultimately this light can never be extinguished.

In what I know now was no mere coincidence, only a few weeks before Susan's passing, I came across a book about mediumship. Intrigued by the idea that consciousness continues after death, I enjoyed the evidence-filled stories of communication with those who have passed. I had no idea that in the very near future, I would have a personal stake in learning more about the afterlife.

Highly motivated to connect with Susan after my epiphany at her viewing, I began to sit quietly each day. I asked to sense her presence like the medium in the book I had recently read. I never expected that my quest to connect with Susan's irrepressible spirit would result in the complete transformation of my beliefs and a 180-degree career change.

While my sole intention in meditation was to find comfort and healing, it soon became clear that my soul had bigger plans. The daily experience of expanded states of consciousness during these meditations awakened abilities that I had no idea I possessed.

A CALLING

I discovered that I could perceive and communicate not only with Susan—a story I relate in my book *Making the Afterlife Connection*—but also with other people's deceased loved ones. Even more surprising to this former naval officer, I found myself communing with beings I had previously disavowed, such as guides, angels, archangels, and spiritual masters.

During these interactive visits, I always asked for information that was not held in my conscious or unconscious mind. Post-session Google searches to validate afterward what I had discerned left me with only one verdict: consciousness is multidimensional and creative, and it exists beyond space and time.

My meditative practice also stimulated the ability to accurately perceive information about family members, friends, and even strangers that no one had shared with me. I would later learn that meditation quiets the activity of the left hemisphere of the brain and activates the more intuitive right hemisphere, bringing the two hemispheres more into balance. Nevertheless, there are still times when I have to remind my husband that I am not a mind reader!

In all seriousness, were it not for the consistently clear and convincing information shared with me in my telepathic interactions across multiple dimensions, I never would have gone public as a medium. However, having learned firsthand how healing and transformational evidence from the higher realms can be, I set aside my discomfort with my new role and embraced what I now acknowledge as a calling.

It was a tremendous honor to serve my country, but today I can imagine no greater privilege than to serve humanity as a spiritual teacher. I know that my naval background and tours of duty at the highest level of the U.S. military were part of a soul-level plan. My unique path brings much-needed credibility to trans-dimensional communication and the spiritual truths about our interconnectedness that it reveals.

OPENING OUR EYES TO SPIRITUAL TRUTHS

One of my most important missions today is to help people understand the problems caused by relying solely on our physical senses to interpret our world. Such a narrow focus causes us to believe that we are separate from each other, from nature, and from our source. When we fail to use the alternative perceptual system of expanded consciousness, we limit our potential for love, comfort, connection, and inner peace.

The result is spiritual blindness, obscuring the deeper truth that we are inherently interconnected and part of a unified whole.

I'm reminded of the time that Ty and I took our friends Mitch and Karen to the Route of the Hiawatha bike trail in western Montana. This scenic rails-to-trail adventure includes 10 unlighted railroad tunnels and seven very high trestles. The first tunnel is 1.66 miles long. Not only is it bone-chillingly cold and damp, it is also completely dark. You can't see the light coming in at the other end for the first 15 minutes of riding.

I had made the mistake of not checking the charge on my bicycle's headlight before leaving home. I entered the tunnel thinking all would be well, but only a few yards into the ride, I found myself nearly blind. I knew there was no turning back, as I would risk running head-on into another cyclist. Unable to see the ground, the walls, or anything but the dim outline of Karen faintly illuminated by her headlight a few yards ahead of me, panic took over my body.

I instantly started praying for spirit to keep me from crashing, and I did my best to calm myself with deep breaths. Nevertheless, my arms shook almost uncontrollably, causing me to wobble like a five-year-old using training wheels for the first time. I shouted to Ty behind me to stay clear as I veered crazily left and right.

When I finally emerged into the welcome sunlight, I felt upset and isolated—everyone else had managed to enjoy what was a terrifying ordeal for me.

The next two tunnels were short enough to allow natural light in from both ends. Still, I was unable to relax, dreading the return trip in complete darkness through the longer first tunnel.

Just outside the entrance to the fourth tunnel, our group paused to take photos. As we put our phones away and stepped back onto the pedals, Mitch called out cheerfully, "Lights on, sunglasses off!"

His words took a moment to register. *Wait! What?! Sunglasses?!* My hand flew to my face and my fingers wrapped around the dark lenses that had been shielding my eyes since we left the parking lot. The blindness in the tunnel was completely my fault.

I didn't know whether to laugh or cry. Too relieved to feel foolish, I shared my lapse in awareness with the group and admitted to the stress I'd been experiencing. Their good-natured ribbing helped me get back into the flow, and we enjoyed the rest of the ride with no further incidents.

At regular intervals for the rest of the day, I questioned my guides in spirit, *Why didn't you let me know I had my sunglasses on?* Normally, they communicate important information in a variety of ways, including helpful thoughts whispered in my ear with perfect timing. In this case, all I had heard was the wind murmuring in the tall ponderosa pines.

Perhaps I was deliberately kept in the dark to share this lesson now. It's not lost on me that my misadventure on the Hiawatha trail provides the perfect analogy to explain why most humans don't realize we are both physical and nonphysical beings: We don't realize that we are walking in two worlds at once, that we "see through a glass, darkly."

This well-known phrase from the apostle Paul refers to the limitations of human perception compared with how we can expect to perceive reality when we no longer view life solely through our physical senses. My adventures in consciousness have shown me that we don't have to wait to arrive at a pair of pearly gates to remove the blinders that keep us believing we are separate from each other and from God.

If you've been feeling disconnected, it's not necessary to endure a painful wake-up call such as a loved one's death to discover the light within and turn it up. You simply need to realize you've been seeing the world around you through lenses that shield you from another layer of reality.

In this book, I will help you understand that you are far more than your physical body. You are an energy-being, part of the dynamic energy-information revealed as consciousness. As physicist David Bohm put it so poetically, we are each aspects of "undivided wholeness in flowing motion."

I internalized this truth after I began to reliably perceive information that could not have come from anything I had learned or experienced. My human BS couldn't explain how nonphysical communication was possible. I found the answers I sought through a multifaceted approach: studying ancient spiritual teachings, discerning deep wisdom in my meditations, and learning about quantum physics.

Today spiritual seekers and science-based researchers are coming to similar conclusions about the nature of reality. The result is what I call 21st Century Spirituality™, in which we appreciate and learn from the intersection of science and mysticism.

We are seeing a long-overdue shift as those in the sciences recognize that matter is not primary in our world. Scientists are leaving behind their outdated materialist perspective and acknowledging that the basic essence of life is consciousness. Religious terminology uses the term *God* to explain this omnipresent force that underlies all creation. Mystics call it *spirit*.

In this book, I refer to *consciousness, awareness, spirit, God, the one field of being, divine intelligence*, and a variety of other terms synonymously. I have mostly refrained from muddying things by capitalizing these words, except for *God*, when they refer to the absolute state of pure being. It's all spirit. It can be no other way when all that exists is consciousness and experience.

Terms like *force* and *field* sound impersonal, but individual experience in expanded states reveals something quite intimate and interactive. The field of consciousness from which these words arise is boundless and limitless. This means that everything within this field is connected, and where there is no separation, we call that love.

Truly, no realization could be more important.

Nevertheless, despite technology that is designed to help us connect more easily with each other, we seem more disconnected than ever. Who hasn't been in a restaurant and seen entire families staring at their cell phone screens or texting instead of talking to each other?

It is my goal in this book to show you a way not only to rekindle your connection with others but also to increase your sense of belonging to something far greater than yourself. I credit higher consciousness for showing me why more people aren't doing so now and how to turn this trend around.

TWO LETTERS THAT MAKE A WORLD OF DIFFERENCE

I was awakened early in the morning not too long ago with an unexpected thought that made my eyes fly open. I turned on my side and excitedly grabbed the pad of paper and pen I keep on my nightstand for moments just like this.

"HEY, SIRI!" I wrote in large, capital letters. And then, as guided, I added a *P* after the *S* and a *T* before the exclamation point, transforming the familiar phrase into "HEY, SPIRIT!" I laughed with joy and a bit of amazement at having never noticed that the addition of two letters turns a common expression into a playful prayer.

In the burst transmission download from spirit that followed, I understood the deeper meaning that accompanied the initial insight. My amusement turned to reverence as I realized that this simple play on words held the power to change lives.

I saw how practices like ceremonies, prayers, and rituals to honor the divine can help us feel more connected with nature, the spirit world, and each other. Unfortunately, most people today are conditioned to turn to the external, physical world when seeking information and answers.

This unconscious habit fuels our disconnection, causing us to trust and interact more with our computers than with our own higher selves. We use artificial intelligence for guidance rather than trusting the one divine mind.

Saying, "Hey, Siri!" is fast, easy, and reliable . . . to a point. But every response comes from data that has been input by a human being into the World Wide Web. A new type of thinking is essential if mankind is to survive and move to higher levels.

Saying, "Hey, Spirit!" acknowledges a source of intelligence that can't be programmed. When you turn within, you connect with boundless consciousness beyond the material world, accessing the *cosmic wide web* for answers that are fresh, insightful, and immensely personal.

Why personal? Because unlike a virtual assistant, spirit is the ultimate source of wisdom. Infinite intelligence knows the answers to your questions before you ask them. That's because you and spirit share the same consciousness. Yes, you are a human with limited awareness, but you are also a soul. As such, you are a direct expression of God.

If you find it difficult to acknowledge this truth, then it's time to question your BS. Better yet, say, "Hey, Spirit!" and question everything.

That's what I started doing after my stepdaughter passed. The result is a life of joy and flow that I never imagined before 9/11 or Susan's transition. It is now second nature for me to make a shift in awareness at random times throughout my day and reap the rewards of consciously attuning to the ever-present inner guidance system.

I call this living The Awakened Way™, and it's available to all who are willing to stretch, grow, and climb out of the suffocating box of "me alone against the world" thinking.

Once you do so, you discover that you are never truly operating solo.

Just as there are cell phone, television, and radio signals all around you now that remain imperceptible due to their higher frequency, there are countless nonphysical, beneficent beings at a higher vibration right now, waiting to assist you. As you will see, gaining their attention and their assistance is as easy as saying, "Hey, Spirit!"

Most people want to believe there is more to life than our human stories. Most have had "no other explanation" (NOE) moments that they are eager to talk about when they trust that no one will laugh at them or think they're unbalanced. In this book I will share some of my favorite NOE experiences along with easy-to-understand analogies to help you trust that a loving source of guidance is ever-present in myriad forms and available for the asking.

Imagine a life where you complete tasks in half the usual time and with greater ease than ever before. Imagine not having to plan every task down to the tiniest detail because you are magnificently guided moment by moment.

This book is a prime example of the kind of flow you can look forward to when you turn to spirit as your trusted assistant and companion. Let me tell you how it came about . . .

With three books published by Hay House, my editor suggested that I should meet Hay House's vice president, Patty Gift, the next time I traveled to New York City. As plans came together for a visit to Manhattan, I was delighted when Patty offered to meet me for brunch at Serafina on Park Avenue.

The high-vibe energy that flowed between us immediately showed me I had met a kindred spirit. This was no formal business meeting. We chatted like old friends as we sipped coffee and enjoyed our meal.

"What's next for you?" Patty asked, and I told her about the documentary that would soon be released about my book *Wolf's Message*. Unfamiliar with the story, her eyes widened when I told her that Wolf was a young man who had been struck and killed by lightning like Susan. After issuing a spoiler alert, I shared the evidence Wolf left behind that proved he knew exactly when, where, and how he would pass.

"Wait until you hear the poem he wrote the day before he died," I said.

Patty listened intently while I recited: "Spirit of great healer, awaken from within this heart. Peace and tranquility, flow like water . . ."

I paused for effect and then emphasized the final line of Wolf's prophetic poem: "The time has come to allow the light of nature to free my soul."

This was a moment I was used to observing as Patty, like countless others with whom I had shared these words, digested the deeper meaning. Predictably, her eyes widened at Wolf's mention of "the light of nature" freeing his soul just before he was killed by a bolt of lightning.

Sitting in that restaurant, the words *peace and tranquility* from Wolf's poem suddenly danced before my eyes. They brought my recent download to mind, and I excitedly announced, "I want to show you something really cool."

I rifled through my purse and found a pen, but no paper. Glancing to my right, I grabbed a paper napkin and wrote "HEY, SIRI!" in big letters. Smiling like a kid with a secret, I left just enough space after the *S* and before the exclamation point so as not to let the cat out of the bag too early.

"I was awakened early last week with an insight that could help people find the kind of peace and tranquility Wolf wrote about. Are you ready?"

Patty nodded and leaned in for a closer look as I strategically inserted the *P* and *T*—the first letters in the words *peace* and *tranquility*—into "HEY, SIRI!"

She did a double take, and her face broke into a big smile as the new phrase "HEY, SPIRIT!" revealed itself. She then leaned back and cocked her head while I excitedly shared how Wolf knew that we as a species are out of balance.

I explained that Wolf's main message is that we put too much attention on the outer world instead of turning within. As a result of worshipping technology and the logical left brain, we lack awareness of our true nature and are not aligned with our souls.

"Wolf came back to me in the reading I did for his parents to share that we need to get out of the head and into the heart."

I pointed to the words on the napkin. "If every time we're about to say, 'Hey, Siri!' we pause, shift awareness to the higher realms, and say instead, 'Hey, Spirit!', the peace and tranquility Wolf prayed for will become our reality."

I grinned, happy to see from the expression on Patty's face that I wasn't the only one who found the turn of phrase enlightening.

"What you just shared . . ." Patty said, allowing her voice to trail off.

Now my eyes widened as I sensed her thoughts and completed her phrase aloud: "Oh my God, it's a new book."

She nodded and said, "Give me three or four sentences, and we'll put a deal together."

Authors who have gone through the agony of compiling 50-page book proposals with chapter-by-chapter summaries, detailed market analyses, promotional plans, and sample chapters will understand the miracle of this magical moment.

I was being spontaneously offered a book contract without being on pins and needles, and without the nail biting while such a proposal made its way through countless committee meetings. This was one of those moments when—if angels were physical beings—everyone in the restaurant would have heard their harps.

Hours later, I sat at the gate in the Newark airport and typed the four descriptive sentences Patty had asked for while I awaited my flight home. One week later—true to her word—an offer for this book arrived in my inbox.

This, my friends, is a NOE story. And you can believe I saved that napkin!

WELCOME, JOY!

Things like this do happen when we believe that we are part of a greater reality. They become almost commonplace when we trust that we are always being guided, and we make a commitment to paying attention to the nudges and the inner voice. This presence can be subtle but has been known to shout to awaken us to one of the great spiritual truths shared by my guides: "When your heart's in the right place, things fall into place."

Once this book revealed itself in my conscious awareness as a done deal, the floodgates opened. Ideas for topics and chapters flowed from my fingers into my laptop on the flight home. They poured out onto my nightstand notepad and into my iPhone's Notes app over the next few days.

This would be my 17th book. For each of the 16 volumes I had written in the past, I followed the same pattern to get organized: I wrote each idea on a separate index card and spread them out on the large surface of my bed. I asked spirit to show me the best order for the concepts to be shared, and then I moved the cards into rows, as guided. The rows became chapters, which, when gathered into stacks, became an outline that guided me through the actual writing process.

I went through the same process this time, but I only got as far as spreading the cards on the bed. As I gazed upon the disorganized checkerboard of paper, I heard a voice say, *Not so fast.*

Confused, I paused and listened. Not all guidance from spirit comes in full sentences. Often, there is simply a knowing. In this case, I knew that if I trusted the process, this book would unfold differently. I gathered the cards back into an unordered stack and put them beside my computer.

The next morning in meditation, I felt the familiar nudge to pick up my iPad. I turned it on and opened a blank e-mail addressed to myself. For over 14 years, I had followed the same process to record the daily Awakened Way messages I received from my guides, Sanaya. At times they spoke as a collective consciousness of unseen helpers. At other times they identified themselves as individuals with a specific voice.

On this morning, the voice was one that I call Joy. I had the first of what I now call "conversations with Joy" in late 2019. I knew then by the powerful presence and the content of the message that this was the highest self with whom any of us is capable of communicating while in a physical body.

Was Joy God? Yes, Joy said, and so are we humans, albeit greatly limited in comparison. Joy explained that Joy was talking to itself for the experience of living through each of us.

We have now come full circle—just like life—back to the teaching I shared earlier about who we really are. This is one of the main goals of this book: to help you understand and accept that there is only one song singing through all of us in this one uni-verse.

Having learned to trust these divine conversations, I surrendered that morning into a delicious dialogue with Joy that showed me how this book would unfold. I saw that it would, indeed, be a different process than my previous writing efforts.

Even though I have amassed hundreds of pages of my conversations with Joy, spirit wanted me to sit when guided and engage in fresh dialogues for each chapter. The practice would serve three purposes:

1. The conversations would convey teaching straight from source.
2. The higher energy present in the words would be transmitted to you, the reader, allowing you to entrain to the more refined vibrations of higher consciousness. This means that your frequency will naturally increase to a higher level to match that of the conversation.
3. Then embodying this new level of being, you will be given the opportunity to say, "Hey, Spirit!" yourself and see what teachings ensue from Joy within you.

IT'S YOUR JOURNEY AS WELL

In other words, you can do this, too, because spirit speaks to and through all souls.

I have divided this book into two parts. In Part I, spirit and I will show you some helpful inner adjustments that will make your connection clearer when you turn within and listen to spirit. You'll learn the types of personal issues that higher consciousness will help you with and how the answers and guidance can come.

I lace my teaching with stories from my own interactions with higher consciousness. They are filled with verifiable evidence that will help expand your personal belief system about what is possible in your own connections with spirit. To that end, I also include a number of practices and tools to help you raise your consciousness and connect more easily and clearly.

How will you know these experiences are not your imagination? We will address that as well, and much more. After teaching countless people to connect with higher consciousness, I know the common stumbling blocks and how to overcome them. More important, spirit knows exactly what you need to learn.

Part II acknowledges that despite our differences at the surface level, we all face similar challenges over the course of our lives. It's how we as a species evolve.

In this second section, we'll address some of the most common issues people ask guides about. You'll read how spirit responded when I requested wise words about dealing with topics such as forgiveness, judgment, disappointment, impatience, grief, and much more.

Then, using the techniques that you learned in Part I, you'll again have a chance to say, "Hey, Spirit!" yourself and see what insights arise perfectly tailored to you in each of these situations. I provide prompts after each essay that will encourage you to discern precisely what will most help you on your journey by turning within for wisdom.

Doing these practices will establish a pattern that will serve you well for the rest of this lifetime and beyond. You can gain the personal experience of being always connected while having the channeled collection of essays from spirit provided in Part II also serve as a standalone spiritual resource you may wish to return to again and again.

It is my hope that by the time you finish this book, you will have had enough practice going within for assistance that you will automatically do so whenever you feel angst, loneliness, anxiety, or any other challenging aspects of the human condition.

I can't promise that you'll experience only joy and happiness after reading this book. Spirit tells us that we didn't come here to be perfect. We came here for the fullness of life, bumps and all. But you will certainly find far more peace and tranquility when you apply what you will find in these pages. You'll find yourself turning to your internal guidance system rather than automatically seeking external sources.

I have discovered that when people come to me for answers from their guides or loved ones across the veil, they already know what they're going to hear. They simply don't trust their own inner knowing that is always and already present because of our innate interconnectedness. Yet, it is possible to learn to trust.

Read what follows slowly and carefully. Much of it will challenge your current way of seeing and being in this human world. But you didn't come here to sit still and stagnate. You came here to stretch and grow. So, dive right in! Do the practices, and you will learn that you don't need a psychic, a medium, a self-help book, or any electronic device to access the answers you seek.

Imagine a life where peace and tranquility flow like water. Imagine a life where you don't panic when you can't find your phone, because you know that you are already and always connected to a source of love and guidance that is eternally yours.

I'm so glad that Joy has led you to this book. As you will soon see, with "Hey, Spirit!" as your go-to, such a life is fully possible.

Sorry, Siri.

PART I

FINDING YOUR CONNECTION

CHAPTER 1

ANNIHILATED

I awoke with my heart racing. I was in full fight-or-flight mode, but for no discernible reason. I knew a panic attack when I felt one, having gone through a troubling period in my mid-20s that resulted in several bouts of identical symptoms.

Fear of the random recurrence of those terrifying episodes led to an ongoing sense of distress and shame that I shared with no one back then. I knew the symptoms were psychosomatic, which bruised my ego badly. Naval officers were supposed to be strong and sane. Gratefully, I outgrew that period through sheer will, no-nonsense self-talk, and stacks of secular self-help books.

Now the long-forgotten feeling of impending death closed in around me as I lay in my bed. It was as if the decades of freedom from those waking nightmares had never happened. But something was different this time around.

In my 20s, I thought that I was destined to endure the frightening attacks alone. I repeatedly asked, like so many do when frustrated and desperate, "What is going on here?" But my questions were rhetorical. I didn't actually expect an answer back then. With no belief in any intended recipient, they dissolved into the ether.

Now I knew beyond any doubt that a team of unseen helpers is ever present, ready to assist me with any challenge. I reacted instinctively, calling out directly and very intentionally to my guides in spirit, "What is this all about? Please help me!"

It took only moments before I heard a response: *Just watch it.*

The words sounded like my own thoughts, but I knew they came from higher consciousness. They had to have a higher source, for I was incapable of finding my own solution while in the grip of such intense anxiety.

The advice seemed absurdly simple, yet in between my ragged breaths I found enough presence to understand why I was being guided to observe my symptoms. Focused so intently on my physical experience, I was held prisoner by *The Story of Me*. Spirit had taught me that a simple widening of awareness from the limited perspective of the ego to the much more expanded point of view of the soul brings instant relief from suffering.

Like an actor moving from a theater's stage to the balcony, I mentally made the shift from experiencer to observer. Detached from the frightening thoughts and feelings, they immediately lost their hold. I watched with curiosity as they flowed through me and dissolved like wispy clouds, leaving me lying in the dark as if they had never happened.

I shook my head to clear the fog and made another direct inquiry: "What was that all about?"

In response, I heard, *You were warned that ego would push back when you try to annihilate it.*

I nodded in understanding as the cover of a book I had been reading earlier that day, *The Mandala of Being*, appeared in my mind. In the book, author Richard Moss described a useful model for understanding our true nature. He encouraged readers to draw a large circle on a piece of paper with a smaller circle in the center. I had followed his directions and continued as instructed, writing the words "Me" and "You" within the shape.

To my surprise, when I turned the page, I saw that Moss had placed these pronouns differently than I had. My diagram had "Me" in the center circle and "You" outside of it, in the larger circle. In Moss's mandala, the small center circle remained empty. "Me" and "You" held equal positions within the outer circle.

For a moment I was confused. Why wasn't "Me" in the center? Didn't we all perceive the world rotating around ourselves from our "center of the universe" point of view? And then I laughed with awareness at my conditioned response. I had fallen right into ego's trap.

In that eye-opening moment, I understood what Moss was so brilliantly showing: "Me" and "You" are what I refer to in my teaching as our "stories." The true center of everyone and everything is the aspect of consciousness that never changes and is beyond our individual experiences: It is pure "being."

Sure enough, when I turned the page again, I found Moss's mandala completed with what rightfully belonged in the center: the two powerful words "I AM." In my mediumship classes, I teach my students to connect with higher consciousness by surrendering their identification with ego and shifting to the part within each of us that never changes. Moss's mandala showed this shift graphically.

In the text, Moss explained that we could replace the words "I AM" with what the 13th-century Sufi poet Rumi called "the Beloved." I have enjoyed many of Rumi's deeply mystical poems and was familiar with his use of the term. Until that moment, however, I had not equated Rumi's Beloved with Spirit. I now understood more deeply that he was referring to our shared, true center when he used this beautiful name for our source.

The beauty of Rumi's poetry contrasted starkly with my guides' mention of annihilating the ego. Suddenly, I recalled reading that when we remove "Me" from the center, we effectively annihilate the ego. Moss had warned that there is often some kind of egoic retaliation as a result.

My eyes widened in wonder. Was the panic attack my ego's way of pushing back because I put the Beloved center stage?

My guides interrupted my musings and gave me a task: *Look up the definition of "annihilate."*

Grateful that my husband, Ty, was out of town and would not be disturbed, I turned on the light. I picked up my iPad from the nightstand, opened a new tab in my browser, and typed in "Dictionary.com." In the search box, I entered the word *annihilate*. I discovered the word means to make void, nullify, or cancel the effect of. It is derived from Latin roots meaning to bring to nothing.

The definition surprised me. I had equated annihilating the ego with killing it. But of course, "Me" is not solid and can't be killed. Instead, we simply return it to nothing through a conscious shift in identity to "I AM."

I recalled how my favorite teacher of personal transformation, the best-selling Hay House author Wayne Dyer, referred to *ego* as an acronym for "Edging God Out." Wayne and I had the chance to chat at length when he came to my house for a mediumship session. Now, I pictured the last time we exchanged e-mails before he passed unexpectedly of a heart attack. He had signed his e-mail, "I AM Wayne."

Staring at the glow of my iPad's screen, I suddenly felt lightheaded. I recognized the disconcerting yet welcome sensation that occurs when a spirit wants to get my attention. With intention, I became hyper-present and was startled to feel Wayne's bright, cheerful personality.

The first time he dropped in on me, several months after he passed, his familiar voice left no doubt who he was. Still, I had put him to the test, asking him to tell me things about himself and his cause of death that were not known to the public. I later called his sister-in-law and validated all that he said, and I delivered a reassuring message about his continuing work in the nonphysical realm.

Do you want proof this is me? he asked now.

I could sense a gentle teasing in his question, so I responded, "Why not?"

You're speaking at a church later this month, and you haven't yet decided on a topic.

He was right, but he wasn't telling me anything I didn't already know.

Aware of my thoughts, he said, *You will speak about courage.*

I frowned. "Why courage?"

Look it up now.

I cocked my head. This night was unfolding like a bizarre dream, yet I was wide awake. First a panic attack, then a lesson about Rumi's Beloved and annihilating the ego, and now guidance from Wayne Dyer for my church talk? Where was this going?

Having learned to trust spirit, I opened Google and did a search for "courage." I clicked on the top result. It opened to a blog post that seemed inconsequential.

Look at the date of the post, Wayne urged.

My eyes moved to the bottom of the page. The blog was published on August 29, 2015.

I recognized the familiar shiver of a miracle in the making. "Don't tell me that's the date you passed."

I felt Wayne smile. *Look it up.*

I clicked the back arrow and put the cursor in the Google search box once again before typing, "What day did Wayne Dyer die?"

I never fail to be awed when those in spirit reveal their presence in clever ways. I had asked for evidence, and he provided it by leading me to a blog post published, indeed, on the date of his death.

He didn't give me much time to catch my breath before saying, *I want you to get my latest book.*

"Now?"

Yes.

A few more clicks on my iPad brought up the sales page for Wayne's last book, *I Can See Clearly Now.* Thankful for the instant gratification of modern technology, I purchased the electronic version and downloaded it immediately.

Go to the last chapter, Wayne directed me.

I followed his orders without question now, just as I had learned to do in the Navy.

Go to the last page.

The sense of knowing that I was being led to yet another wondrous gift welled up. I swiped left multiple times until I came to the end of the last chapter. The final words appeared to be two lines of verse.

Minutes earlier, a palpable experience of detaching from ego-based fears had left me breathless. Now my breath caught for a different reason. The web of consciousness glistened before my eyes in this undeniable demonstration of the interconnectedness of all life.

Wayne Dyer—still very much alive in spirit—had guided me to a lesson in his final book taught to him by none other than the poet Rumi:

Love has come and it is like blood in my veins and in my flesh.

It has annihilated *me and filled me with* the Beloved. (emphasis mine)

❁ ❁ ❁

The story I relate above is what I call a "no other explanation" (NOE) moment. There is no other explanation for these synchronistic events than that the Beloved manifests as all of us in one interconnected web of life.

We are all spirit—the I AM state of pure being—arising as consciousness taking form. This Aware Awareness experiences life through the stories of "You" and "Me." When I first began to understand how we humans fit into the grand scheme of a greater reality, it was stories like the one I just shared with you that took me outside the confines of my "only human" worldview.

Now, thanks to such NOE experiences, I can state with complete confidence that nonphysical beings are as real as we are. The ability to communicate with them is not a gift reserved only for certain people. With commitment and practice, you can learn to bypass the brain's filters and access alternative states of consciousness.

That is my intention for you. Better said, that is spirit's intention. The conversation with Joy that follows speaks of annihilating the ego. As Joy transmitted these words to me in meditation, I realized that I couldn't include them in this book without telling the backstory. Instantly, I knew that was Joy's plan all along—to begin the first chapter with this evidence-filled example of our connection with higher consciousness, followed by relevant and necessary initial teaching that comes straight from the highest level possible.

Read the dialogue below deliberately slowly. There are often double meanings and subtle humor in these deep conversations. Truly hear and take in the information that is being shared. Make sure you understand what is being conveyed line by line before moving on.

And don't just read the words. Notice how they feel as you experience and process them through your energetic heart.

All words carry the frequency of the source. Be aware of a shift in energy as you digest these special dialogues through your nonphysical senses. Open to receive the gift they carry of not just spiritual wisdom but the transmission of a higher vibration that will increase your own ability to say, "Hey, Spirit!" and personally access guidance more easily.

A CONVERSATION WITH JOY

(Words from spirit are italicized. All others are mine.)

I sit for my morning meditation. My intention is to connect with my guides and receive their daily message. Instead, I feel a now-familiar shift in vibration and know what is about to happen. A conversation with Joy begins before I finish my second deep breath . . .

It is through this practice that we have come to know each other.

Is there another way?

Many, but this (sitting daily to commune with spirit) *is the one that reaps the most rewards.*

Why is that?

For you must make a choice to set aside your precious time and sit.

How important is intention?

All-important. If you sit (in meditation) *simply to lessen your stress, that relaxation will result, but little else will change, for the root cause of the stress has not been addressed.*

Root causes. They're often deeply hidden.

Exactly. And the root cause of all your challenges is when you forget that we are one.

But we're not the same.

We are the same, but you experience diminished quality and quantity of awareness.

That's another word for you, isn't it: Awareness.

It works for the active aspect of being, but the root of awareness is . . .

Being.

You've got it.

And sitting in the silence allows us to experience "being" for ourselves. Most people don't know what it's like to simply be.

It is one thing to sit quietly. It is another experience altogether to sit silently and just be without filling in the blanks after my name.

After "I AM."

Yes.

The brain does that . . . fills in the blanks with stories such as, "I am sad, I am happy, I am a male or female."

Before the story was, I AM.

Wow. If only people understood this.

You did not.

Until I began searching for Susan, sitting quietly and saying, "Reveal yourself to me."

And she did not do so as you expected.

You're right, but that's when you showed up.

In my many forms (as other spirits, guides, angels, and masters).

Correct, but I didn't know that for quite some time. At first, I thought I was making up the people and beings I sensed.

How else am I going to show up to you except as images or word-thoughts that don't come through the senses?

We call that our imagination.

What you call imagination is consciousness arising through means other than the eyes, ears, touch, and so forth.

But most of us feel that those sensations, thoughts, and images are limited to our own mind.

*Yes, that is what happens when you do not yet realize that there is only one mind, compart***mental***ized—note the word "mental" within this word—into what you call "my mind" and "your mind."*

What is your definition of mind?

I will have to put it into words that you will understand, for "definition," by definition, means to ascribe meaning to something, and meaning arises through personal experience.

That's deep.

As is the mind . . . a deep well of sensations, thoughts, and images—the content of experience—that has no bottom. It is like a spring whose contents bubble up endlessly from a hidden source.

Wow. Best definition of mi— wait! You corrected me just now without even using words: Best *experience* (versus definition) of mind that has ever come to mind!

I see you did not say, "My mind."

Yes. I'm remaining aware of the power of words and using the power of choice to hold on to a higher understanding of how this all works.

It works any way it may, for there is no one way of being once I move beyond pure being.

And every one of us in human form is you, spirit, being "something" other than just "being."

Bingo.

Saying "Bingo" takes me back to (my book and movie) *Wolf's Message*. That word came up several times in that story with great meaning.

In this case, "Bingo" is not referring to a game, but is an expression said when one hits a target dead center.

Why did you choose the term *dead center*?

For as you have learned in meditation, when you return to center and experience pure being without adding anything after the basic awareness of I AM, you may have annihilated ego, but you are far from dead. This is the awareness that will change your world.

And as you have taught me so magically through the experience with the panic attack, Richard Moss's teaching, and the visitation from Wayne Dyer in spirit, "to annihilate" something does not mean to kill it.

Correct.

It means that we return what we perceive as "something" to "no-thing."

Yes. Ego is the story . . . all that you have added through experience to I AM.

We call our experiences "things" and give more power to them than to being, yet science has shown that no "thing" is really solid or permanent.

"Being" is permanent, if from the use of this word, you infer that it never dies.

So, coming full circle (pun intended), we return to meditation as a means to get to know ourselves beyond the story. And in so doing, we get to know ourselves as you.

But I AM not simply meaningless, storyless "being."

I know, but I didn't know this when I first started trying to connect with Susan.

What did you discover?

You want me to put it into words!

Yes, for those still addicted to the story aspects of LIFE (love in full expression).

Okay. I discovered that all of us are you: I AM . . . God—which is not a thing or a person, but a state of being . . . consciousness—expressing itself or yourself through stories.

Correct. And take that one step further.

So I am you playing the story of Suzanne. And Susan is you playing the story of Susan.

Better said, I AM experiencing life through all of you.

And meditation allows us the personal experience of this undivided flow. Of the connection.

See for yourself.

I have, but not with my physical eyes.

Eyes open or eyes closed, the view is the same for me.

I am grateful for the expanded view you have offered to me.

It was your choice. I have always been within view.

Out of my desperation to connect with Susan.

Whatever it takes, sooner or later I wake up in my stories.

Does the story ever end? People are afraid that those they love will dissolve back into you, and they will never see their loved ones again.

Understandable when you think that all you are is the story of you and your loved one, but here we are, and I AM not going anywhere.

For all there is, is here-now.

Yes. Here I AM. And what love has joined together—what stories I have sown—no physical death can tear apart.

Thank you so much for this teaching.

You are so very loved. It can be no other way.

YOUR TURN

What questions has this chapter raised for you? Some will likely be answered in the coming pages, but why wait? Hold on to the expanded state you're experiencing now and find some paper and a pen. When you're ready, write "Hey, Spirit!" at the top of the page and follow this by writing out the first question you want answered.

Next, relax, slow your breath even more, and simply listen for whatever words come into awareness. Understand that you can't make these conversations happen. They arise by grace as you allow your path to unfold with the timing that only the divine knows.

If no answer arises, spend this sacred time watching how ego tries to step in and derail your efforts. Don't resist this (ego loves when you fight back). As the guides advised me, *Just watch it.* All those ego sensations, thoughts, and feelings will simply dissolve like clouds when you notice them and let them go without judgment.

When you do hear words that pertain to your question, write them on a new line. Let the dialogue flow as it will. Pay no attention to ego's thoughts of whether you're making it up. We'll dive deeper into the topic of discernment in a later chapter. For now, just enjoy the process.

CHAPTER 2

AAH . . .

How does it help to know that everything is spirit? Does life suddenly get easier? Yes and no. You still have challenges—they are part of life on planet Earth. But you no longer give them as much attention as you did in the past. You have moments of suffering, as all humans do. But in the more awakened state, the inner observer kicks in, and you remind yourself, "It's a story!"

From this state of heightened awareness, you are far more empowered to make choices from the soul's perspective that will lessen your suffering. You remember that you are never alone. You then pause long enough to call out, "Hey, Spirit!" whether that be to loved ones who have passed, guides, or other higher beings.

Just ask my friends Patty and Dave Hart how it changed their lives to learn that we are eternal beings. When we first saw each other face-to-face on a Zoom call, a gray pall filled their auras. And no wonder. They had endured an agonizing year of watching their beloved daughter, Lauren, deal with acute lymphoblastic leukemia. Lauren succumbed to the deadly cancer three years prior to our meeting, and the grief clearly had taken a toll.

In that Zoom session, Lauren proved beyond any doubt that she is still very much with Dave and Patty. Their emotional healing was immediate and visible.* After hearing so clearly from their daughter, Patty admitted, "I feel like this tremendous weight is gone. I no longer feel guilty because she isn't here to feel the joy." Patty understands that Lauren doesn't want them to suffer. She and Dave are traveling again for the first time since Lauren became sick. They live life more fully now, knowing that Lauren moves forward with them in spirit.

My assurance that everyone can learn to connect with higher consciousness propelled Patty on a spiritual journey quite different from her Catholic upbringing. Using my simple SIP of the Divine® practice, where "SIP" stands for "Sit in Peace," Patty began setting aside a few minutes each day with the clear intention of connecting with Lauren herself.**

Following my instructions, each day she closes her eyes; relaxes fully with a few slow, deep breaths; and invites her daughter to draw near. As Patty notices her normal thoughts arising in the mind, she allows these to drift past. When she senses Lauren's presence or something unexpected or surprising occurs, whether when doing the SIP of the Divine or during normal waking consciousness, she engages her daughter in conversation and asks for validation.

---

* See the transformation for yourself. The complete, unedited reading is available to watch on my YouTube channel: "Actual Evidence of the Afterlife: A Complete Mediumship Reading with Evidence, Photos, and More," posted May 27, 2024, by Suzanne Giesemann—Messages of Hope, YouTube, https://youtu.be/xGM-4-EzvaM.

** My SIP of the Divine meditation is explained in detail in my book *The Awakened Way*.

The request is merely a formality. As you will hopefully come to experience, the greatest evidence of a loved one's visit is your own unmistakable sense of knowing, centered in the heart. Nevertheless, asking for a sign is a fun way to keep the momentum going, and Lauren has sent some great ones that have left her parents astounded.

I'm thrilled that Patty experienced a true breakthrough in connecting so soon after committing to this daily practice. These periods of meditation have also afforded Patty the chance to come to know her own expanded self. This became evident to me when she and a handful of other close friends offered to read a draft of this book. After receiving the first chapter, Patty admitted with great excitement that she felt drawn to review it more than once.

"Each time I've read the chapter," she said, "I am struck by a new understanding of I AM. The definition of *annihilate* brought a clearer understanding to me of how letting go of ego isn't a violent thing, but more of a gift to our soul. It allows space for I AM to be present without the complication of our story."

Patty told me that when she was a child, her family would take her to church every Sunday. Her father always quizzed her and her siblings afterward to make sure they had listened to the sermon and understood it correctly.

"With all of my religious background," she wrote in an e-mail, "I never knew God. I knew of Him—a man named God—and a man named Jesus, and all the saints, and that there was a place called heaven that we go to when we die. I was taught that I need to be a good person and not commit sins, and then I will go to heaven. But everything was always SEPARATE!"

I could feel Patty's excitement even without the capital letters as she continued, "What I now know as God, Source, Spirit, Beloved, and Joy is that it is EVERYTHING! We are part of all that is good and sacred. To know this and to truly believe this changes everything! We are ONE! To also know that we are never not connected to I AM and to experience the wholeness of being fully aware is such a gift."

Amen!

I hear comments like Patty's quite often from those who are questioning the long-held beliefs of personal stories that are passed down through generations about the nature of God. Over the years, I have given the keynote address several times at the annual conference hosted by the International Association for Near Death Studies. On one of these occasions, a volunteer pulled me aside to thank me for my work. The man told me that he had taken one of my classes and received a clear, convincing, and helpful message from a loved one across the veil.

My jaw dropped when he told me that he had served for 40 years as the pastor of a Pentecostal church. In my experience until then, those with more fundamentalist beliefs are often fearful of personally talking to spirit. He admitted that his parishioners were equally surprised by his participation in my class. One of them asked him, "Doesn't mediumship conflict with Christianity?"

I laughed with joy when the pastor said, "I told them that mediumship is Christianity with the walls blown out."

Yes! It is not blasphemous to admit that you are the outbreath of God. There is a part of you that already knows that all of us are being breathed by our common source. Everything else—the many ways in which we differ—is story. When we identify only with our community and beliefs that have been passed down without question, we fortify the walls of illusory separation.

It is interesting but not surprising for me to see how even those most faithful to their religion's rules and creeds are willing to set them aside and consult a medium when someone they love dies. Fear based on passed-down doctrine loses its grip when a person is mired in grief.

But how does awakening to your true nature help in dealing with the normal day-to-day challenges of being human? Once again, when you come to know that you are so much more than your story, then peace, tranquility, love, and joy become the norm.

Just after I began to write this book, I received an e-mail from Sophy Burnham, a friend who is one very wise soul. She is the *New York Times* best-selling author of *A Book of Angels* and numerous other highly engaging works dealing with spirituality and metaphysics. Sophy asked if I would be willing to read her latest manuscript for a possible endorsement. I paused for only the briefest of moments, aware that my own writing project left little time for granting favors.

But Sophy was the first person to show Ty and me that Susan is still with us. She doesn't advertise the fact that she is a medium, but our reading with her changed our lives.

We had not told Sophy in that very first meeting who we wanted to hear from, yet she sensed a young woman in a brown uniform who stood in front of us. Having no idea that Susan died from a lightning strike, Sophy described a tingly, electrical feeling running up her arm. She complained of suddenly experiencing "the headache of Zeus and Athena," the Greek mythological god and goddess associated with thunder and lightning.

This would have been convincing enough, but then Sophy utterly rocked our world. She casually reported that this young woman in spirit had brought with her a baby boy whom she wanted to introduce to us. Sophy had no idea that Susan was pregnant with a boy when she was killed.

I would do anything for Sophy.

So I happily agreed to review her book *The Wonder and Happiness of Being Old*. And I'm so glad I did. She knows better than most humans who we are as souls, and she expresses this in a most delightful, non-didactic way in her new book.

I found her words exceedingly encouraging for those of us who notice every new wrinkle as the years pass. I made time between other tasks to digest a few pages every chance I got. I even read it while on my elliptical machine three days in a row. Halfway through one workout, I could no longer contain my excitement and simply had to share it with my closest confidante.

"Call Lynette Setzkorn," I said aloud to Siri while pedaling. (There *is* a time and place for technology!)

Lynette is a dear friend who has been on the spiritual path with me since her sister introduced her to my work in 2012. When Lynette and I met, she used crutches to walk.

A double knee replacement would have removed her intense physical pain, but she was so terrified of dying that she refused to have surgery. She hadn't traveled by air for over 30 years out of fear that if her plane crashed into the ground, her soul would continue going straight down to hell.

In response to tremendous family trauma early in her life, Lynette had spent a few years as a bit of a "wild thing." But that wasn't why she thought she was destined for damnation. It was the frightening BS passed on from leaders in her childhood church that doomed her to decades of misery. She was sure there was no place for her in heaven, having been taught from age five to recite, "Woe is me, a poor miserable sinner."

Thankfully, 12-step meetings led to salvation from her self-destructive behaviors, but they did not completely quell her lifelong terror of hell. The complicated grief from her husband's early death and her beloved father's passing only added to her deep emotional pain.

Thanks to her sister's urging, exactly one year after Lynette's husband's transition, Lynette watched my documentary *Messages of Hope*. That, she claims, is when her life changed. She dived into learning all that she could about mediumship and the greater reality. She and our mutual friend Brenda followed me to in-person events around the country, declaring themselves my number-one stalkers.

This, coupled with countless readings from mediums and lengthy discussions with others on the same path, revealed to Lynette an afterlife that was far from the fire and brimstone experience she had been taught to fear. She described the result of her efforts in her deeply insightful blog, *An Unexpected Mystic*:

> *I could see clearly a reality I'd never really considered before. And then my own STEs (spiritually transformative experiences), and making the direct connection with my loved ones confirmed it was all true. It was transformational, beyond anything I could have imagined at First Lutheran, or even in what came after . . .*
>
> *What a gift I was given when my husband died, and daddy shortly thereafter. We are forever and I know now what I did not then.*
>
> *Out of desperation, I chose YES, in a willingness to consider something beyond this world, something that caused old friends to roll their eyes and dismiss me as crazy from grief.*
>
> *As a result, what I once thought might kill me, has proven to be the single greatest gift of my life. Unbearable pain and sorrow and emptiness have been left behind. Choosing YES has brought me to living fearlessly, with the certainty that love doesn't die with the last breath, that life really is eternal, even for people who aren't perfect (which is all of us, of course).*

> *I can see clearly now, and it's beautiful. My greatest wish is that every one of us could find that same peace, that same knowing.*
>
> *In AA we used to tell people, "if you just can't believe there's any kind of a higher power, believe that I believe and start there."* *

This is sage advice from a woman who now racks up frequent-flier miles and goes hiking and biking on her two new titanium knees.

On this day, when I got so excited reading during my workout, Lynette answered my phone call immediately. With the familiarity of good friends who can dispense with formalities, I bypassed a greeting and said, "You are absolutely going to love Sophy Burnham's new book!"

Both Sophy and Lynette are gifted writers who draw in readers with their descriptive, heart-based prose. But it was more than good wordsmithing that Lynette would appreciate. I knew she would resonate with Sophy's positive take on aging.

Indeed, Lynette squealed with glee when I told her the topic.

"I love being old!" Lynette exclaimed. This was obvious to me when she turned 67 and began bragging to everyone that she was already 70.

I told her that the book did not paint our older years as completely rosy. Still, Sophy had done a magnificent job of showing that this time in our lives can be one of continued growth and greater peace.

Lynette let loose one of her joyously infectious laughs and said, "Oh Suzanne, contrast that with a group of retired women I just found on Facebook. They're all complaining about the same things they did when they were thirty!"

---

* "I Can See Clearly Now," *An Unexpected Mystic* (blog), September 23, 2023, https://anunexpectedmystic.com/2023/09/23/i-can-see-clearly-now/.

"Like what?" I asked.

"They're moaning about their men, and jealousy, and competition from other women . . . how they look, how other women look, why others won't do what they want, and on and on and on. It's insane!"

Lynette is not normally one to judge. She and I have indulged in countless conversations about the human tendency to compare ourselves with others. Now she caught herself and concluded, "They just don't get it."

And this, we both knew, was not a judgment. It was an acknowledgment that when we get caught up in our stories, we suffer like the women in the Facebook group so clearly continue to do. As some believe Einstein asserted, insanity is doing the same thing over and over and expecting things to change. When we complain year after year about the circumstances in our outer lives without exploring and developing our interior lives, nothing changes.

Whether at 30 or at 67, the stories of "me and you" keep us trapped in "only human" behavior. Sophy Burnham, at 86, was able to write a story about the wonder and happiness of being old because she "gets" that we are more than our stories. Lynette is joyously celebrating her 70th birthday three years early because she has blown the walls out of what had been a most tumultuous story.

The human brain is programmed to focus on the outer, objective world. It takes what the senses feed it and cherry-picks select details—generally the most dramatic ones—putting them into stories, whether true or fictional. Once we come to know that there is a better way—the Awakened Way—we make a conscious choice to shift beyond the drama and say, "Hey, Spirit!" In so doing, we find the peace that is always and already here.

A CONVERSATION WITH JOY

Note: Once again, please don't just slide right into reading the lines that follow. Pause for a moment or more and take a relaxing breath. Remind yourself that what you are about to read is imbued with a higher vibration than the last few pages. Settle awareness into the heart area, and when you are ready to be truly present, en-Joy . . .

Joy, when I say, "This is consciousness," it has a different feel from saying, "This is spirit."

Yes.

"Spirit" feels more alive.

It is merely the difference between science and spirituality.

And if I say, "This is God" . . .

That is the religion component.

You show up in so many different ways.

I AM all the ways.

Of course! And whether we're speaking in terms of science, spirituality, or religion, it really is all a *dance* of energy and information, isn't it?

I do not like to be still. It is why I created all that is.

But why do we have these conversations where I am talking to you, and you are talking to me? Why don't I just sit here and know what you want me to include in the book?

Try it.

Okay . . . (I pause to just "be.") Well, when I do that for a few moments, the mind rises up.

Not exactly. You say, "The sun rises," but it only appears that way from your human perspective. The mind does not rise any more than the sun does. I, spirit, rise up and I become the mind. Put another way, the mind is a container for the rising waves that are experienced as sensations, thoughts, and feelings. Mind temporarily gives the waves of ST-F (pronounced "stuff") a container to hold the experience of these waves.

I understand that when you say "container," you don't mean the brain. You're simply using an analogy . . . a concept of the mind as the entirety of the waves we experience.

Correct.

But why can't we just be still?

Stillness is our natural state.

Our?

Yes, me, and you as me.

Okay.

Again, stillness is our natural state. Yet there is so much fullness in stillness that we simply cannot sit still, just like little children who are forced to sit in a chair. They begin to swing their legs, and then the fidgeting spreads to the torso, and you know the rest of this scenario.

Yes, I know it all too well. It's restlessness.

Indeed. That is why I create you as an experience moment by moment as something that appears separate from my state of simply being: to satisfy the restlessness arising from this ever-present, infinite potential. One can only sit in the chair so long until One jumps forth and plays. But playing alone can get lonely.

And so you create "us."

Yes, in all my myriad forms. And I do not just arise as what you call people, you know. Start a list. Begin with what is beyond the tip of your so-called nose. What you perceive before you in the room is not "man-made" in the deepest sense. All that you see and experience from your human perspective is me—spirit or consciousness—in expression. First came spirit, then came human, then came the room with all the furniture. You are used to going outward and explaining the world with an outward object focus (OOF!) as if you humans are the ultimate subject, the ultimate creators of what is in the room with you now. Ultimately, there is only one subject.

You . . . "This" . . . awareness.

Yes. And there you have it. Or better said, here you have it: Consciousness. Awareness. Spirit.

Do I call this "God"?

You may, and perhaps in doing so, you will now release some of the restrictions you have placed upon spirit with this man-made label.

Aren't all labels man-made? Wait! You just explained this. All arises first and foremost from spirit!

Now you're catching on. This is the "always already here" (AAH!) *view instead of the outward object focus (OOF!).*

Ah, yes, AAH versus OOF! No wonder we are all so stressed all the time. We keep focusing on the stories and all the drama. OOF! It can be exhausting.

Correct. Seek "AAH!" by letting the waves subside, and experience peace . . . tranquility . . . flow.

Peace and tranquility—the *P* and the *T* missing in "Hey, Siri!" Thank you for this lesson.

Thank you, my dear one, for turning within instead of moving awareness outward to what has already been created. "Fresh is best." It behooves you to remember This.

I love how you speak so often in double entendres. It does behoove us to remember that we are "This" . . . Always and already here.

That is correct. I AM . . . This . . . "The One to turn to"—the ultimate subject of all that is. But do not revere me. That returns you to the "God as separate" mindset—knowing now that mind is a limited thing with boundaries—instead of remaining more and more in a state of flow.

Removing the boundaries . . . blowing the walls out of my BS.

A most excellent exercise.

YOUR TURN

Have pen and paper ready to use and enter an expanded state of consciousness with a few deep, slow breaths. Begin by saying, "Hey, Spirit, please show me how my focus on the outer, objective world is keeping me from knowing my true self."

Hold the intention of receiving unexpected insights about one or more of your current challenges. Write whatever arises in the mind that stands out from your normal ST-F.

Whether or not you have a meaningful experience, notice the peace that is Always and Already Here as you allow the mind to settle down.

AAH . . .

CHAPTER 3

RESISTANCE

Stephanie Pfennig sat in the back row of the hotel ballroom in Reno, Nevada, where I was teaching my Personal Mediumship Plus class. The goal of the workshop was to teach people how to better connect with their own loved ones, whether they considered themselves a medium or not. That was the "personal" part of the course's name.

The "plus" in the title referred to my emphasis on the spiritual lessons that result from communicating with spirit. I help students understand that mediumship is possible because we are not separate from our source and aid them in moving beyond their resistance to this concept. As in all my classes, I laced my teaching with evidence from the greater reality to demonstrate our deep interconnectedness.

During the final exercise of the two-day workshop, I guided the participants in a meditation to connect with a loved one and write what they sensed as it occurred. Stephanie had registered for the class in hopes of contacting her two children across the veil. Her daughter, Katie, passed at age 22 in a tragic hiking accident. Three years later, while her grief was still raw, her stepson Nick joined Katie in spirit.

Stephanie found my work by searching for hope. Literally. She had been a spiritual seeker for years, but her daughter's death left her in need of consolation and healing. When she entered the word *hope* in a search box, Google brought up my name. I credit Katie and Nick for the string of events that followed.

Stephanie very clearly felt her daughter's presence during that classroom exercise. Still, like most people in the early stages of opening to spirit, she questioned whether she was making up what sounded like her own thoughts. Nevertheless, she followed my instructions and wrote the words she heard verbatim on her notepad: *Mom, you're gonna love your new job.*

Stephanie had worked as a business consultant and project manager for 33 years. She longed to leave the corporate world and do something that would allow her to help people who were grieving. She hadn't yet figured out how she was going to do that and still pay the bills.

She and her friend Christa, whose daughter Avery was also across the veil, had by that time co-founded the nonprofit KAREfarm to honor their children. Steph and her husband, Mike, repurposed some rural property they'd bought years earlier and developed KAREfarm into a healing place for those in grief to gather in nature and commune with others who understood what they were going through.

These special retreat weekends served the stated purpose beautifully, but not in a way that would allow Stephanie to quit her corporate work. When Katie referred to a job during the exercise, Stephanie thought she was referring to a new business client that Steph would soon be taking on.

As sacred as it was to feel her daughter's presence, the exercise brought a sense of disappointment. If she took on a new client, it might be years before Steph could do something more satisfying for her soul.

As the workshop came to an end, Stephanie noticed a line of people forming in front of me—students who wanted to talk or have a book signed. To her surprise, she felt a sudden urge to approach me and ask if I needed help on my staff.

Not normally one to impose herself on others, she shook off the idea and began gathering her belongings. The impulse persisted, but Stephanie resisted it. To her surprise, the pressure became so intense that she was sure she was going to be sick to her stomach.

By this time, my husband had arrived to help me pack up my equipment. As usual, he brought our two dachshunds to lavish love on my students. Seeing the dogs, Stephanie decided that a chat with Ty would settle her stomach until she gathered the nerve to approach me.

I was unaware of Stephanie talking with Ty until he called out across the room, "Hey, Suzanne! Stephanie had a red dachshund named Rudy!"

I looked up in surprise and delight. Our beloved red dachshund, Rudy, had crossed the veil a few years earlier. We loved that little boy like a child and continued to say goodnight to him every evening when we turned out the light.

By this time the room had emptied except for a few stragglers, and I approached Stephanie. We chatted about our two Rudys and discovered more stunning similarities, not only in our pups but also with our children across the veil. Stephanie then paused and stiffened noticeably. She cleared her throat and told me that she was feeling guided to offer her services to my team.

I have received similar kind offers from other members of our Awakened Way community over the years. Usually,

I thank them and make a note of their name. Stephanie's proposal came at just the right time, because I had recently been thinking about bringing on board another assistant.

We joked that our daughters and our dachshunds must have brought us together, but now I see that this was indeed the case. Stephanie began working with me shortly thereafter, and she has been an immense gift both personally and professionally.

Her first task was to help with the launch of my book *The Awakened Way*. She later admitted that she was nervous because the other members of my team had been on the spiritual path far longer than she had. To get up to speed as quickly as possible, she began doing the practices from the very book she was promoting.

I later interviewed Stephanie on the topic of dealing with grief for an episode of my Awakened Way podcast. In that show, she described my BLESS ME® Method of connecting with higher consciousness as a game changer. The practice took her to a discernibly higher level of clarity in connecting across the veil.

Stephanie shared during the show that a good friend named Christi had passed a year earlier. Using the seven-step BLESS ME Method, she reached out to Christi in spirit and immediately sensed her friend step into her awareness. To be sure this wasn't her imagination, she did as I advised in the book and asked for a sign. Without pause, the image of tiny marshmallow Peeps popped into her mind. This was followed by the face of Christi's sister Beth, who was also a friend of Stephanie's.

Feeling somewhat foolish but hoping to validate the visit, Stephanie later called Beth and asked if Peeps held any significance for her and Christi. To Steph's delight, Beth responded enthusiastically that peeps were their "thing." From childhood well into adulthood, the two sisters did funny things with Peeps to make each other laugh. They hid them from each other, they exploded them in the microwave, and they racked up enough other unusual Peeps tricks that Stephanie clapped her hands with joy. Her corporate mind could now accept what her heart already knew: She had successfully connected with Christi.

Stephanie's meditation practice was doing for her exactly what it does best: It was quieting her left-brain activity and heightening the sense of unity and connection that lies latent in the right brain. The left hemisphere of the brain is programmed to resist change. It relishes routines, structure, and predictability. The right hemisphere is all about flow.

When I retired from the Navy, the two hemispheres of my brain were not at all in balance. The regimentation of military life and my highly detail-oriented assignments led to a seriously left-brained focus. My commitment to daily meditation after Susan passed tipped the scales in a very positive way. While maintaining the strong organizational skills that helped me in my military career, I brought online unforeseen abilities that complement routine tasks.

I had not realized just how much I've learned to trust my right brain's contributions until Stephanie became my chief of staff. I recently entered into a short-term contract with a team of bright social media experts half my age. They came to my awareness when I was invited to address a local Women in Business group. Before I gave my remarks, each woman introduced herself and briefly described her work.

As I listened to these enthusiastic entrepreneurs, I thought about my own work. *Hey, Spirit!* I said silently. *I could really use someone to help me with my online presence.*

The thought had not occurred to me at any point prior to that moment. This is how I know, in retrospect, that spirit put that request in my mind to help connect me with

Emerald Briscoe. She was the next woman to stand after I reached out to spirit. You can imagine my surprise when she announced that she worked for a social media company!

A few days later, I met with Em and her partner, Key Ronholt of AMAVI Social, at a local coffee shop. We sipped on cappuccinos as they shared ideas about how they might help me spread my messages with more innovative posts. As we wrapped up the discussion, Emerald confirmed my suspicions about spirit's intervention.

"I had been sitting at that meeting wondering if it was just a waste of my time," Emerald admitted. She told me that she had been a member of the women's group for a while, but she had not garnered a single lead from her networking efforts. "I told myself that I wasn't going to attend any further gatherings if nothing came of it, and then you called."

I nodded in recognition of a setup from spirit. Before we left, I asked them to submit a proposal for their services. I didn't tell them that the request was a formality. I loved their enthusiasm and their vibe. The decision was completely an "energy thing." Indeed, their proposal, when it arrived, was as professional as I knew it would be, and we signed a contract.

I was surprised later when Stephanie admitted that she learned even more about the Awakened Way from my method of hiring Key and Em. "What do you mean?" I asked, suddenly appalled that I had acted spontaneously and hadn't thought to bring her more into the hiring process. "How would you have done it?"

"Well, in the corporate world," Stephanie replied, "we would have identified at least three potential companies. I would have written up a list of requirements and a set of evaluation criteria. I would have the candidates do presentations about their proposals, and when we chose one, we'd negotiate . . ."

My laughter interrupted the rest of her description. "I'm sorry I steamed full speed ahead with this, Steph. I guess we should have done some of those things, but I didn't feel any resistance at all when I tuned in to Key and Em. They just felt right."

Stephanie laughed with me, and we agreed that both methods have their benefits. Balancing the left and right hemispheres for a state of flow is the key to success. In the end, what we really want is a happy medium. (I'm sorry. I couldn't help that.)

In hindsight, Stephanie and I see that she had indeed tuned in well to Katie in that Nevada workshop exercise when she heard, *Mom, you're gonna love your new job.* Katie wasn't referring to a corporate client at all, but to the way her mother would be helping spread the messages of hope that mediumship brings.

Learning to balance our human roles with our soul's expanded presence takes commitment and awareness. You are here to be fully human, but don't forget that the inner guidance that your soul mediates is always and already here.

I'm grateful to Stephanie and my other assistants who willingly offered to review the draft pages of this book. After Steph read the first conversation with Joy, she told me that she used my BLESS ME Method to do the "Your Turn" exercise. She offered to send me what she wrote.

Pleased that she took my recommendation seriously and was open to doing the practice instead of just glossing over it, I eagerly read her dialogue. I immediately recognized fears that are common to many who are new to the concept of oneness. As you will see, completing the process proved quite helpful in alleviating the anxiety that some of the spiritual concepts in the chapters evoked.

I was grateful to see that Stephanie thought to say, "Hey, Spirit!" and seek guidance to alleviate her discomfort. Equally gratifying is the response she received. It's clear that the wisdom shared came from beyond her conscious mind. It stands as a beautiful example that all of us can connect with spirit, no matter how experienced we are in doing so.

With Stephanie's permission, I share with you now her dialogue with spirit . . .

STEPHANIE'S CONVERSATION WITH SPIRIT

Hey, Spirit, why does going back to the I AM scare me so much?

(An image of the Statue of Liberty comes to mind.)

The I AM gives you freedom from the notion that you have to do this world by yourself, that you are struggling alone. You are not.

But I don't want to lose my individuality . . .

(An image of a tall apartment building with many units comes to mind. The sun is shining brightly upon it.)

The infrastructure holds the building together; the stairs allow travel to and from the various apartments where different people live (or the multiple incarnations of the whole). The pipes supply water, a life force to each apartment/person. The furnace provides heat and cooling. I AM is the infrastructure, the pipes, the stairs, the beams, the light provided for each instance of the one infrastructure that sustains the individuals in the apartments.

How can I not feel sad that Katie is not solely my daughter, but perhaps also other things to other people in different lives? It would feel to me like this teaching is nullifying or invalidating such a sacred bond I have with her.

Imagine if you felt this deep and profound love you feel for Katie for everyone on this earth? Can you imagine the peace we would have if all did the same?

Yes, that's pretty awesome, but it still wouldn't feel so special and unique.

Look up soul groups.

(When Stephanie looked up soul groups later, what she read gave her comfort that the souls in our group are with us across many lifetimes. The material emphasized that the purpose of the group is to help each other through various lifetimes to learn and grow together. She resonated with the idea that her children and other significant people in her life are indeed "special." She envisioned them "having each other's back" across many lifetimes.)

What you give at KAREfarm is a fraction of how you feel for Katie, and even that fraction is changing lives.

(An image of the sandbox she played in as a child comes to mind.)

You played in the sand, created roads, structures, and infrastructure for a make-believe world in which you played with your people figures. You do that here on earth also.

Is there anything else you can tell me that will lessen my resistance to this notion of not being *me*, but one with all?

(The image of a bird's nest with three eggs in it comes to mind.)

The nest is home (I AM) to the individual eggs. If the egg cracks, the yolk would flow back into the nest. If the egg remained unbroken, it would hatch as individual birds.

Stephanie abruptly ended her written conversation here, but the various analogies had helped her make sense of the concept of oneness.

I asked if she felt she was making up the words as she wrote them.

She replied, "I'm starting to understand when the information is likely coming from me or from spirit. I get an immediate image of something before any words or knowing comes. Then I ask spirit to tell me more about what I just saw."

This is when she received the deepest insights. The words flowed with a sense of knowing that arose from a higher level than in her normal state of waking consciousness. She also found the advice surprisingly practical, as spirit used everyday things like apartment buildings and their components to help her relate better to them.

This element of freshness and surprise is a key indicator that spirit is directly inspiring you with the insights. Another way to distinguish spirit messages from imagination is when long-buried memories unexpectedly arise. In Stephanie's case, the image of the sandbox took her to experiences she hadn't thought about in decades.

"That sandbox was a special place where we kids spent hours and hours creating little cities with our play people," she wrote. "My father built that sandbox, so the imagery also made me feel really grateful for my mom and dad who supplied that for our childhood."

She then expressed her thankfulness for the opportunity to do the exercise. It served the purpose of alleviating her resistance to the concept of oneness. She now understands that when it comes to spirit and its many forms, creation is not a matter of "either/or" but "both/and." In other words, her daughter Katie and all of us are both spirit and human. We do not dissolve permanently into nothing when spirit no longer breathes life into our bodies. We are eternally both spirit and the ongoing stories it weaves.

And this is what turning within to commune with spirit is all about: finding healing, comfort, and guidance that we can't access in our ordinary states of consciousness.

To that end, I invite you to use the seven steps of my BLESS ME Method that I describe below for connecting to higher consciousness. I devised it with spirit's help when I decided to teach mediumship. While connecting with spirit is a natural ability, students truly appreciate having a reliable system to create the optimal state in which to interact with those in the nonphysical realms.

The seven steps are designed to do this in such a way that you flow easily from one step to the next without the mind wandering. Experienced meditators praise the method for helping them drop into expanded states quickly and easily and achieve their meditative goals with greater consistency. It is an excellent practice when you have more than the few minutes it takes to do the SIP of the Divine meditation.

The time spent in the preparatory phases of the BLESS ME Method will afford you deeper and often unexpected adventures in consciousness when you say, "Hey, Spirit!" and turn within.

Enjoy!

YOUR TURN

THE BLESS ME METHOD OF CONNECTING TO HIGHER CONSCIOUSNESS

Note: Any time you sit to do the practice, set a clear intention. Do you wish to connect with a loved one in spirit or a guide or an angel? Do you have a question for spirit for which you seek the highest possible answer? Do you want to train your mind to be more still? Do you wish to revisit challenging experiences from your past and heal them with the help of spirit? The method works for all these goals and more.

Set aside time when you won't be disturbed. Sit or lie with your back straight and arms and legs uncrossed. Flow through the seven steps as follows:

- **B = Breathe**
  Begin with three long, deep, vagus nerve breaths, inhaling very slowly to the count of four and exhaling to the count of six. The added two counts put pressure on the vagus nerve, helping activate the body's relaxation response. As you take these three breaths, silently state the kind of suggestions a hypnotist might use, such as, *I am sinking deeper, deeper, deeper.* Scan your body for any tension after the third breath and release any remaining tension. Move on to the next phase only when you feel fully relaxed.

- **L = Lift Your Vibration**
  Get a sense for how those in the spirit world might view your energy field based on how you are feeling mentally and emotionally. Is it bright or dull? The goal is to remain in this stage until you are shining brighter in an

energetic sense. This stage can take seconds or minutes depending on how light you feel going into it. Tools that will help you lift your vibration include:

- ◊ Thinking of something you are grateful for and generating true feelings of appreciation
- ◊ Thinking of someone you love with all your heart and feeling the love
- ◊ Visualizing the light of your soul in your heart and turning it up as bright as possible
- ◊ Moving awareness through each of your seven energy centers (the chakras) and visualizing them clear, bright, and balanced
- ◊ Sharpening all your nonphysical senses by remembering a place in nature that you love and then seeing, hearing, smelling, and sensing all the details present there

- **E = Expand**
  Imagine how your energy field (your aura) looks to those in spirit now that you are relaxed and have lifted your vibration. Sensing the circumference of this torus or doughnut-shaped field, use a strong exhale to expand the boundaries to infinity. Let yourself hear your breath and travel with it as you fill all of space.

- **S = Surrender**
  Acknowledge that you are a soul temporarily in a physical body, and this is what makes soul-to-soul communication possible. Willingly set aside your ego and your identification as "only human" by stating, "I surrender."

- **S = Shift**
  Imagine you are holding a remote control that will allow you to experience the perfect frequency for the dimension you wish to connect with in this meditation. Knowing that consciousness flows where attention goes, state, "Shift." This is akin to pressing the desired dimension's channel on your remote control. In so doing, trust that you are now aligned with the necessary frequency to attune to higher consciousness.

- **M = Merge**
  Invite a nonphysical being to blend their energy field with yours. Do so with enthusiasm, and radiate love outward. Use whatever words help you express your heartfelt desire for communion, such as, "Come now," or "Let's dance!"

- **E = Experience**
  Be still. Set all expectations and assumptions aside. Sit quietly as you listen, look, and notice what arises in awareness. All ST-F (sensations, thoughts, and feelings) will float through the mind like clouds passing through a pristine blue sky. Let them do so until something stands out. At that point, trust that this fresh energy is from spirit, and engage it. Raise whatever questions come to mind. Ask for clarification. Dialogue or simply sit back and experience whatever spirit gifts you for your benefit.

  Note: Should you at any time feel fear, simply observe with detached curiosity. Send love to the sensations or thoughts and affirm, *I AM the light.* Darkness cannot exist in the light of love.

Remain in the Experience stage until the meditation naturally ends. Send a wave of gratitude to spirit for whatever you have gained. Take a refreshing breath, wiggle your fingers and toes, and return to normal waking consciousness.

CHAPTER 4

SNAGS AND SIGNS

A funny thing happened as I wrote about Stephanie's friend Christi in the last chapter. One of my newest assistants, also named Christy, came to mind. That's not so strange. After all, it's easy to think of someone when you read or hear a similar name. What caught my attention was a "knowing" that I would be writing about Christy in this next chapter.

I call these moments when something stands out and catches our attention with our sixth sense a "snag." It's a useful tool that nonphysical beings can use to get through to us when our human minds are focused on the objective world. But we must be present enough to detect the snags. The good news is that once we agree to be snagged and we start playing along, they are easier to notice and happen more often.

Most people know not to pull a snag on a sweater. The opposite is recommended with snags from spirit. When something unexpectedly catches your attention, and it comes with a "look closer" feeling, you want to pull the thread. You do this by pausing and acknowledging that spirit may have a message for you embedded in whatever it is that just lit up your awareness.

This is the time to say, "Hey, Spirit, why did that just snag me?" Ask with unwavering trust that someone at a higher frequency has prompted this question and is standing by to answer. And then turn within and scan your awareness for something novel and insightful coming to mind that is related to whatever snagged you.

As I tuned in to why spirit wanted me to include Christy in this chapter, I sensed I was supposed to tell how she came to work for me. I'm chagrined to admit that just like when I brought my social media team onboard, I made an instant and intuitive hiring decision with Christy. Happily, I could clearly see spirit at work in bringing us together.

My friend Lynette had recently announced her desire to retire from being my podcast producer and content creator. She was ready to get out from behind a computer and do some traveling before she actually turned 70. When I realized she was serious, I silently said, *Hey, Spirit! Please help me find the perfect person to fill Lynette's shoes.*

At the time I issued this request, Lynette was assisting me while I spoke at the Helping Parents Heal conference in Scottsdale, Arizona. We were rooming together at a house that I rented near the event venue. Midweek, we met for lunch at our favorite Phoenix hangout, Pita Jungle, with our beloved friend Lisa Wilcoxson.

You wouldn't know from Lisa's peaceful demeanor and beautiful smile that she has endured great tragedy. Her only children, Michael and Anthony, are both across the veil. While many with such a burden would turn bitter, Lisa transmuted her grief into a life of heart-based service to others. Today she is an outstanding evidential medium whose abilities I greatly respect.

While enjoying caramelized cauliflower with extra tahini sauce for the third day in a row, I was inspired to ask Lisa if she knew of someone who might be interested in helping me produce my podcasts. She paused and did what I recognized as a "Hey, Spirit!" move. Instead of looking downward and furrowing her brow, she moved her eyes up and to the left, softened her gaze, and stared dreamily into space.

After a few moments, her voice took on a note of curiosity as she reported, "I keep hearing, 'Christy, Christy, Christy.'" Then her eyes locked onto mine, and she announced, "She's perfect!"

Lynette and I leaned forward, knowing that whatever Lisa was about to share was going to be good. She excitedly told us about Christy Majors, a dear friend and member of Helping Parents Heal who lives near her in the greater Phoenix area. "She's a fantastic artist and is super creative. Her daughter, Tess, is across the veil, and Christy has a great connection with her. Christy really 'gets' what your work is all about," Lisa said, nodding her head with certainty now. "No wonder I keep hearing her name. You'll love her!"

When people and events come together in magical ways, we call this "flow." It's a prime indicator that you are aligned with spirit. Lisa pulled out her phone and texted Christy on the spot. I recognized a spirit setup in the making when Christy responded immediately and agreed to meet us at our house the next day.

The energy between the four of us during that initial get-together was electric. I resonated with Christy's bubbly personality immediately. As an added bonus, I sensed her daughter, Tess, in the room celebrating our meeting.

Christy told me that she discovered my work in 2021 when, in the early stages of grief, she came across one of my YouTube videos. She began listening to every recording of mine that she could find and knew from the start that she was going to meet me.

The feeling that we would come together persisted for Christy at the Helping Parents Heal conference in 2022 when I presented a keynote address. Further indications soon followed. Lisa Wilcoxson's husband, Rick, made a slideshow for that event to honor the attendees' children across the veil. On large screens across the front of the ballroom, hundreds of portraits appeared in rows of three that scrolled one after the other to the accompaniment of evocative music.

Christy's heart caught in her throat when her daughter's beautiful face appeared on the screens. To her surprise, when the row of photos scrolled up, Tess's image was followed in the same spot by the smiling face of my stepdaughter, Susan. By then, Christy understood how our children across the veil work together to let us know they are here. She saw the juxtaposition of their photos as a sign that she had been introduced to my work thanks to the efforts of Tess and Susan.

When I discussed the possibility of joining our team, Christy enthusiastically agreed. I shouldn't have been surprised that she had the talent, the time, and the willingness to take on what would be a completely new endeavor for her. Even though we know how spirit works, the four of us marveled at how the web of consciousness had revealed itself yet again.

Christy and I sealed the deal with a hug during that initial get-together in Arizona. It was only later that I realized just how perfectly spirit had set us up. As I got to know her better, I learned that Christy's husband, Inman, is also an author. Was it merely coincidence that one of his many novels, *Wonderdog,* features a dachshund like my beloved Rudy on the cover? And where do Christy and Inman live? Why, on Red Dog Road, of course.

Christy caught on to her job quickly. She has a strong intuitive sense for sorting through the archives of my webinars and choosing just the right clips for new YouTube videos. This week, she sent me an e-mail with two new choices for my approval. As I watched the first one, I realized that we were being set up by spirit once again.

I picked up my phone to call Christy. "I'm sorry to tell you this," I said when she answered, "but I can't use one of the videos you sent."

Most people might be a bit miffed when told that their work is not usable. Christy merely laughed, intuitively sensing a God-wink in the making.

I was quick to explain, "I'm supposed to write about the content of that video instead of putting it online."

"Okay . . ." she said, pausing as if waiting for the punch line.

I told her that earlier that morning I'd been snagged by a book on my bedroom bookshelf. Pulling the thread, I picked it up and recognized it as one written by a woman I had featured on my podcast two years earlier, mystic Mary Reed. Shifting awareness to my guides, I asked why Mary's book was special. I didn't discern any specific reason. I simply sensed that I was meant to know the book was there.

Now I said to Christy, "You can imagine my surprise when the cover of that same book showed up just now in the video clip you chose."

"You're kidding!"

"Nope," I said. "You were used."

I told her that I had completely forgotten about a God-wink that occurred between Mary Reed and me after a particularly powerful conversation with Joy. With more than five years of monthly webinars from which to choose excerpts, Christy had zeroed in on the story about Mary Reed and her book and had chosen it for the week's upload.

"It makes a great video clip, but it's also perfect for my new book."

Now giggling, Christy said, "I have to tell you, Suzanne, I was kicking and screaming the whole time I was editing that clip. I knew I was supposed to choose it, but I also sensed that we weren't going to use it for the upcoming podcast. My guides kept saying, *Chill out! Trust the process.*"

"Well, now we know why," I said, laughing along with her. The snag with Mary's book showed us that this was spirit's plan all along.

Pleased that Christy enjoys such a clear connection with her nonphysical helpers, I hung up the phone and headed for my laptop to share the story that follows.

Two years earlier . . .

Busy thoughts interfered with my efforts to settle into my morning meditation. Images of Mary Reed and her new book kept bubbling into my awareness. I was scheduled to interview Mary, and instead of emptying my mind to meditate, I found myself musing about her online courses.

Knowing that I wouldn't be able to still my mind until I made a note, I reached to my side and picked up my iPad. I opened Gmail and sent myself a message with the subject line "What is Mary teaching?"

I hit Send and was about to put the iPad aside when a wave of higher energy passed through me. Feeling a conversation with Joy coming on, I opened a second blank e-mail and again addressed it to myself. I began by writing what was most on my mind:

"Mary and I have been called mystics because we wish to know ourselves more as you. Please help me with this."

You cannot know me more than you do now, for I am all of you. This is what you do not realize in the moments when you become so fascinated with all that we have created outside of you, but everything is a projection of my mind, which you have mistakenly believed is your mind.

So how do I relate to you? And even as I asked that question, you showed me a cell in my body, and you advised me to take the perspective of the cell.

Yes, shall we do it together? For there is no other way (than to do everything with source).

Okay, I am a cell. I am coursing through a highway, which from my perspective of sitting in this chair, I know is a bloodstream. But from my cell point of view, I'm only aware of movement within boundaries that appear like a tube.

Do you see how already you have a higher perspective from sensing outside the cell and inside at the same time? Now shift perspectives and be only the cell.

Okay, now I simply *am*. I'm pulsating and feeding on what is exchanged from outside my boundaries and protecting what is within them. I automatically react when an antigen tries to penetrate my boundaries. I resonate with others like me. There's a friction when I encounter a cell that is not like me. I simply do my job, nothing more or less.

That is correct. And now you are stuck, because until and unless you shift your perspective higher beyond the limited awareness of the cell, you cannot relate further with higher levels. Now relate to the cell from the Suzanne level without going any higher.

Okay. Now I know I am this body and that this body is made up of trillions of cells. I see each cell doing and being exactly what they just showed themselves doing from their limited view. From their perspective, only they exist, doing their job and just being, but now I have this higher perspective. I know that they cannot exist without me. They also cannot exist without the many other systems inside of me. I see that the systems are important to be aware of . . . the interconnections. You are telling me now to visualize this self known as “Suzanne” as analogous to you, Spirit, and the cells analogous to human beings. But that would require the cells to have far more sentience.

One day they will. For now, humans are my creations that can be aware they are expressions of me. Humans are beings who sense the interconnections and co-dependencies. Do you see the main point that, like the cell, you exist within me and because of me?

I do. I cannot exist without you. I am part of you, and I have my being because of you. Now you’re showing me a ladder of sorts. It represents a stepping up of consciousness that is necessary to understand wholeness. And you just instilled in me the awareness that I am not merely thinking through this analogy . . . I could not conceive of the concept of something higher than me if it was not part of me already. So the question still remains: How do I relate to you?

Understand that the higher mind is part of you, but beyond your understanding at the moment. Know it, be satisfied to simply flow, and allow me to do what I do best. The cell does not worry. It does its function. You have higher functions. You are aware that when you act on loving thoughts, you function better. So do that. Trust the higher level to coddle you and nurture you and ensure that you can do what you came here to do: to express me in human form. That is all you need. You have the intelligence to know that you are the highest order of me within the earthly experience. The cell does not know this. Trust me and flow within your boundaries.

Do we pray to you? Is it helpful? Is it a good practice?

You may pray if you wish. It works. And it works even better when you realize that as you relax, I can feed you insights to help you realize your prayers. I can feed you insights to help you return to trusting the higher intelligence that is breathing you. I can help you flow within your boundaries like the cell flows within the boundaries of the bloodstream. You can relax and see every being around you—every creation—arising from me and no longer judge them as bad. You shrivel up when you are tense and judging.

You're showing me a raisin.

It is an apt analogy. When you do not trust spirit, you contract just like a raisin shrivels. Relax. Let down your barriers and soak up the nutrients like the cell does. I am feeding you from my higher state all the time, just as your body is feeding its cells. There are layers and levels of systems taking care of you, just as you do in relation to the cells of your body. The higher levels [guides, angels, archangels . . .] *know they are part of me. They know we are one. Not all humans will understand this while in physical form. But with transmissions like this and soaking up this energy, you have the capability to come into greater resonance with the higher levels. Soak up these nutrients—the energy, this frequency—and accept your divinity. Those of higher frequency do not try to control me or manipulate me. And they certainly do not make the mistake of operating in isolation, thinking they are separate from anything. This separation consciousness is what turns you into a raisin.*

I would love to have a raisin sign today to validate that this conversation is not my imagination.

Do you think it will happen?

I'm lacking the knowing. Wait . . . You just showed me how the spirits in my readings always use apt analogies. So the knowing is flowing in now that the raisin analogy was very deliberate. I get it. I was in "raisin mode" when I doubted that I would get a raisin sign today. Doubt comes part and parcel with fear.

Fear is born of separation. Flow comes with trust and relaxing into the knowing. Trust and knowing go hand in hand.

I'm so grateful for this experience. I wish to be a large, plump, juicy grape, full of sweetness.

And so it is. Do you see how a bit of playfulness resulted when you relaxed? The more you surrender into the experience of being a cell in my body, the more Joy-us is your experience within that body.

And when this journey in a body ends, I return to full awareness of you. Why can I not have the awareness of the fullness now?

For I am so enjoying being you.

Oh God, I feel the love flowing into me as you say that. It makes me want to cry.

Tears of joy.

Wow.

Yes. Wow. This is why I am being you. Do you get it? You are fulfilling Joy's greatest wish, for I so love when we enjoy these moments of aware connection. They are precious to me, made all the more precious because you have moments of ignorance. Do you see?

I do now, and I thank you. May we please talk more like this again soon? I have missed these conversations.

I have not. I am having millions of them all the time. And yet this one is precious here and now. I could not have had it without me being you.

Yes, we matter. Our lives have meaning.

Indeed they do. Carry on, precious one in seven billion. You are all equally precious to me. May all of you see all that is in this manner and shrivel not. You are so very loved.

As abruptly as the conversation began, it ended. My guides stepped in without missing a beat and dictated their daily message. I sent it to myself in yet another e-mail and left my meditation room filled with gratitude.

Following my morning routine, I went directly to the living room to update the Awakened Way app with the fresh spirit message. Ty stood across the room in the kitchen grilling bacon for breakfast. As I sat on the couch and pasted the daily message onto my website, I noticed a song by country singer Luke Combs coming through the stereo speakers. My ears perked up. Was that a snag? Was I going to get my raisin sign through this song?

Eager to validate the conversation with Joy, I opened a web browser and did a search for the song's title. I found the lyrics and shook my head when my eyes got to the bottom of the page. Of course there was no mention of a raisin in a country song. I had broken the unspoken rule of asking for signs: *Don't go looking for them.*

With snags, you are meant to trust the process and wait for them to appear. If the interaction with spirit that you are trying to verify was valid, you will be led step-by-step—no matter how unwittingly—to the wondrous moment when spirit drops the agreed-upon sign into your lap.

I closed the browser. Hearing Ty cracking eggs into the frying pan, I realized I had a few more minutes while they cooked to check my other e-mails. When I opened Gmail again, I saw the earlier message I had sent myself at the bottom of my inbox with the subject line, "What is Mary Reed teaching?"

I quickly did a Google search for "Mary Reed mystic." Her website appeared as the top result. I clicked on a subheading labeled "Courses" and went directly to a page displaying two of Mary's offerings.

Intrigued, I scanned the description of the first course shown. As my eyes took in the words, a wave of knowing traveled from my toes to my torso, and I found myself holding my breath. The heightened anticipation proved well-founded. There, on a website that I was checking out of what I thought was simple curiosity, was the sign that I had asked for. Mary Reed's class entitled "Divine New Being" promised to take students' awareness "from the size of a raisin to the size of a planet."

I fell back against the couch and closed my eyes. There was no other explanation for finding this mention of a raisin than that spirit had set me up from the moment the thought initially occurred to me to check out Mary's courses.

Did I really need a sign? The content of the conversation with Joy and the way it had flowed were proof enough to me that it was genuine. Even more telling, however, was the sense of oneness I experienced while caught up in the flow of words. Still, the exhilaration of finding what to me served as undeniable proof that spirit is in charge was all part of the Joy of alignment.

The next day when I sat to meditate, feeling especially connected, I picked up the conversation where we had left off . . .

Joy, yesterday was amazing with that raisin sign.

It is indeed fun, and I do enJoy experiencing excitement through you. There was awareness that you would find a raisin example.

Well, there was that doubt at first.

Simply human ST-F, born of separation and past disappointments. Keep the past where it belongs. With the fun comes learning and greater trust. Keep it up. Literally. Keep awareness up, not constrained. You asked for a miracle, and you found it in a raisin. Do you see how it does not require me to move mountains to prove to you that I am here? See wholeness and know it is all me, yet do not forget that the human aspect of you will never wrap your mind fully around me. So be content to wrap your heart as fully as possible around all that is. Then, as you do this, you will experience more and more of me. You have been pushing me away, or as so many say, "edging god out." Ego does love to edge me out by labeling, rejecting, comparing, overcoming, superseding, name-calling, judging.

I no longer wish to do that. I wish to—

Be the presence of love that you are, dear one. Then you need have no fear. This connection is a light that never goes out. Where once there was doubt, now there is knowing that this inner glowing is your birthright.

Infuse me with the knowing of this—the visceral awareness—that all is you in equal measure.

It can be no other way. It has always been this way. The comparisons and a lifetime of "more than" and "less than" have kept you in separation consciousness.

Please take it away. I . . . I was about to say, "I am a lowly cell." Forgive me. I fell right into that trap.

Not a trap. A rut. I will help you smooth out the ruts by practicing holding me in awareness.

I feel I cannot do it without you.

You do nothing without me.

Yes, of course. All of us are you.

Now you're talking. Just be love and spread it around liberally.

YOUR TURN

I'm thankful to spirit for showing up as Lisa Wilcoxson, Christy Majors, and Mary Reed in this wondrous web of connections. When you see with the eyes of the soul, you become better skilled at connecting the dots that lead to exactly what you need when you need it.

What connections will unfold for you as a result of being snagged by this book? If you wish to work more closely with spirit, grant permission to be snagged whenever there is a message you need to receive. To set a clear intention, close your eyes; settle your mind with some slow, deep breaths; and move awareness to the heart. Say the following or use your own words:

"Hey, Spirit! I am ready to work more closely with you. I am asking you to catch my attention using any object or sound in my objective awareness. I promise to be alert for these snags and to pull the thread by pausing to ask for clarity. Thank you so much for helping me remain in greater communion with you in this way."

Don't hesitate to ask spirit to validate any interactions you experience. You can ask for a specific sign or request to be given one. In either case, don't actively seek out the sign. It will appear in a way that you can't miss when spirit wants to get your attention. It's all part of the Joy of living a life of flow!

CHAPTER 5

WHO'S DRIVING?

The challenge with habitually seeing only through our human eyes instead of those of the soul is that our default perception is that of separation. Without realizing how interconnected we are to those in this world and beyond, we too easily fall into the trap of judging and categorizing people. This results in seeing some people as more important than others, rather than recognizing that every person is unique and equally valued in the eyes of spirit.

Having spent 20 years in the military—an organization where human interactions are regulated by rank and hierarchy—I certainly understand social stratification. But these tendencies affect all aspects of society. Allow me to illustrate this with one of my all-time favorite jokes:

During a recent visit to the United States, the pope had some rare free time, so he decided to check out the local area. When he walked out of his hotel, his limo was waiting at the curb. Seeing the pope approaching, the chauffeur opened the rear door. Instead of getting in, the pope said to him, "You know, I'm tired of riding in the back seat. Today, I want to drive the car."

"But Your Holiness . . ." the driver protested politely.

The pope gave a dismissive wave of the hand and invited him to enjoy the ride.

Not wanting to insult his boss, the chauffeur took a seat in the back while the pope got behind the wheel. The pope smiled broadly as he pulled away from the curb, glowing with a renewed sense of freedom.

Within a few minutes, they came to the on-ramp of an expressway. Now the pope decided to really have some fun. He could barely contain his excitement as he pressed the accelerator and watched the speedometer climb to 100.

Suddenly he heard a siren. Glancing in the rearview mirror, the pope saw a police car with its lights flashing drawing close behind the limo. He also noticed the chauffeur sliding down in the back seat with his hands over his face.

Not one to let power go to his head, the pope obediently pulled over and rolled down the window. He smiled politely as a patrolman approached the car.

"Sir," the police officer said, "do you know how fast you were—"

The officer's voice trailed off when he looked inside the car. He paused to gather his thoughts and then stammered, "Sir, if you'll excuse me for a moment, I need to make a call."

Stepping to the rear of the vehicle, the police officer unclipped his radio from his belt and toggled the station. When his sergeant responded, the patrolman described the reason for pulling over the car.

"What's the problem?" the sergeant asked. "You know full well that anybody driving a hundred miles an hour gets a ticket. There's no question."

"Yes, Sarge, I do know that, but there's somebody really important in this car."

The sergeant scoffed. "I don't care how important he is. Write him up!"

"No, Sarge, I mean, he's *really* important."

"Come on! Who is this guy?" the sergeant asked with disdain, "The mayor?"

"No, Sarge, the patrolman replied, shaking his head, "He's way more important than the mayor."

"Oh, come on. Who do you have there? The governor?"

"No, Sarge."

Now the sergeant hesitated. "Don't tell me you pulled over the President?"

"No, Sarge, it's not the President."

"Nobody's more important than the President," the sergeant replied. "Seriously, who is this guy?"

The patrolman's voice took on a tinge of awe as he answered, "I think it's *God*!"

There was a moment's pause before the sergeant replied, "God?! What makes you think this guy is God?"

"Well," said the police officer, "It must be God, because his driver is the pope!"

I hope you enjoyed that story. It never fails to get a big laugh when I share it in my workshops and presentations. Humor is an excellent tool for aligning with the higher realms. It opens us more fully to the present moment, helping us transcend artificial barriers such as status and rank. It reveals our shared humanity and allows us to acknowledge and honor our common challenges.

I recall sitting with family members in the common area of the Marine Corps barracks after my stepdaughter's funeral. We had just endured the most difficult day of our collective lives. As we each shared our favorite stories about

Susan, we experienced the heavy mood slowly lifting. It was impossible not to smile and chuckle together at the memories of Susan's sparkly, spunky soul.

This was less than 24 hours after I howled alone in my car and then sought solace from my sister-in-law, Lynn. Now, thanks to the love we all felt for Susan, we found relief in the laughter.

Susan's passing catalyzed my spiritual journey. My efforts to connect with her after her death helped me understand that we ultimately all share the same mind. Your soul already knows this. It's simply a matter of waking up . . . of becoming lucid within the relatively dense state of consciousness we experience in this earthly dimension.

The challenge with waking up is that even though we share the one field of consciousness, we are quite obviously differentiated into individual, sovereign beings. Reconciling this paradox is part of the spiritual journey.

It helps to see the world like those in the higher realms do. Those in spirit tell us that they don't put people into any kind of pecking order like the characters in that joke did.

Yes, there is a hierarchy among our nonphysical helpers, with angels being "higher" than spirit guides and archangels higher still, but this is based upon the ability to beneficially influence greater numbers of people here and across the veil. Because those in the higher realms are aware that all are light beings arising from the same source, their power doesn't go to their heads (so to speak).

Of course, in our human roles, there's good reason for granting greater authority to those with more responsibility. Separating humans into higher and lower positions, however, can bring out some of ego's less desirable traits.

I experienced this from day one of my Navy schooling when I keenly felt and shared the fear of my fellow officer candidates. If we didn't immediately acknowledge superior officers with a sharp salute or use the proper titles and words of respect toward them, we risked being called out and reprimanded in front of our peers.

I sensed this same underlying anxiety in the midshipmen I taught years later during a tour of duty at the U.S. Naval Academy. When my husband, a retired four-stripe captain, would come to visit me on the campus wearing civilian attire, the midshipmen paid little attention to him. By then, I was a mid-grade officer. The only thing the midshipmen focused on when Ty and I walked together were the gold stripes on my uniform. Their salute came first, and not all of them even acknowledged Ty.

I couldn't fault them. They were operating 100 percent in human mode. I doubt they gave much thought to oneness at that time in their lives, but they might have found a modicum of peace if they had understood that we were all playing roles.

When assigned to the Pentagon, I saw two-star generals stiffen and stammer in the presence of my four-star boss. I understood why they were intimidated. I occasionally felt daunted by my boss's gruff demeanor, but the job demanded that I appear confident.

Had I known then that we humans are actors on our earthly stage, I would not have experienced such self-imposed stress. I would have imagined my soul stepping onto the balcony of this theater in the round and asking the general's higher self to pass me the popcorn. Instead, I spent an inordinate amount of time and effort thinking through everything that might go wrong and trying to stay one step ahead of my boss.

Sound familiar?

One of the most mortifying yet comical scenarios from that assignment occurred at the end of an especially long workday at the Pentagon. Each evening the general and I went through a highly ritualized routine to get him from the building into his limousine for the short trip to his private quarters. The process might have seemed absurd to an observer, but it honored decades of tradition and military discipline.

On this day our ritual was interrupted by the general's driver, an army sergeant. Normally I was the one to alert the driver when departure time neared. Instead the sergeant called me twice in 10 minutes to ask if the chairman was ready to be taken home. After his third call, I chided him by asking if he had a hot date. He denied any such engagement.

I peered through the peephole in the chairman's office door every few minutes until I finally saw him gathering his paperwork. I called the driver and told him it was time to pull the car up to the River Entrance. Following our ritual, I wordlessly entered the general's office and retrieved his uniform jacket from the closet nearest his desk. After helping my perfectly capable boss to put it on, I then picked up two briefcases full of his evening's reading material and silently followed him out the door.

It was only a short walk down the hallway and past the security guards outside to the parking lot. The sergeant had pulled the chairman's black stretch Lincoln Town Car to the curb at the bottom of a set of wide stone steps. The general paused while I set the briefcases on the sidewalk and opened the heavy, armored, right rear door for him. When he settled into his seat, I gently closed the door.

Per our routine, the sergeant had already raised the trunk lid. I retrieved the heavy briefcases, walked to the back of the car, and placed the first one in the trunk. I was about to set the second one beside it when to my horror the car began to move. I shook my head in disbelief. The sergeant knew full well that after I closed the lid, I still needed to return to the rear passenger door, come to attention, and bid the chairman goodnight with a crisp salute.

At the time of this incident, I had been in the Navy for 18 years. Duty was highly ingrained in my psyche. As the car pulled away, I thought of nothing else but completing my mission.

Instead of waiting for the driver to realize that the trunk was still open and stop the car, I leaped into action. I began running after the limo—a feat made somewhat difficult by the glossy black pumps and narrow skirt of my dress blue uniform.

The orphaned briefcase became a weighted Frisbee as I flung it into the trunk. I lunged at the lid, caught it with the tip of my index finger, and slammed it shut as the limo picked up speed.

I stared after the retreating car, fuming, until it receded from sight. I then returned to my office and gathered my own belongings as I waited for the phone to ring. Ten minutes later, having dropped off the general at his quarters, the driver called me. He apologized with great sincerity.

Holding back my anger, I told him that I had only one question: "Did the general see what happened?"

"Well," the sergeant replied, "he might not have noticed if I hadn't said, 'Sir, the commander is running after the car.'"

My shoulders slumped and I let out a soft moan before asking, "What did he say?"

"He barely glanced up from his newspaper," the sergeant reported, chuckling now, "but he said, 'That's okay. She's a runner.'"

I'm grateful that I was able to see the humor in the moment. The story makes me laugh to this day. It also shows me how caught up I was in my human role at the time.

Do you have stories of running after your own goals (perhaps not literally, as I did) that came with unintended consequences? Have you ever chased after success or sought approval because you felt something inside you wasn't good enough?

I hope you're beginning to see that what's missing when you do silly human things is the awareness that you are already whole and complete. You can't see this when fully identified with your human character. Thankfully, as you get in the habit of calling on spirit more often, you will awaken to the divinity within and honor yourself as equally as you do those around you.

One of the greatest benefits of meditative practice is gaining all humans as equal manifestations of God. It is truly liberating to greet others with divine love instead of instantly judging and comparing. The latter is learned behavior that becomes a habit. If left unobserved and unquestioned, such habits can last well into later life.

As I think back to those heady yet stressful times as the chairman's aide, I now see how my experiences accompanying the general to events around Washington in that limo provide an excellent spiritual analogy. I would ride in the front passenger seat while the chairman sat directly behind me. He occupied himself by reading reports or making phone calls. He rarely spoke to me, but when he did, it was usually to issue an order.

Much like my work today as a medium, I served as the general's intermediary. I acknowledged whatever he requested and passed it along as appropriate. Just like in mediumship, this required me to remain quiet yet alert, actively listening for directions from a higher level.

The driver had his own orders and carried them out unless otherwise instructed. He didn't need me to tell him to turn right or left unless I or the general gained new information that required changing our destination.

Fixated on my human role, I couldn't view our interactions from a higher perspective. Looking back now with a wider lens, I appreciate the dynamics in that limo for the lessons they provide. Perhaps you can see that:

- Your body is the vehicle for consciousness to experience life in physical form.
- Your personality is driving the car.
- The soul is riding shotgun—a most supportive position!
- God is in the back seat . . . not separate from us, but fully along for the ride.

What if you are receiving advice from the metaphorical back seat from one with your best interests at heart? What if this higher authority sees a bigger picture that can help you make better choices? And what if, instead of insisting on turning one way, you listen to the gentle commands and end up in a better place than you expected?

Few people like being told what to do. The desire for self-sovereignty is yet another built-in aspect of the left brain's programming. But when we say no to what life presents us, resisting what is, we block the flow of guidance that will make our lives easier. Resistance is a sign that ego is gripping the wheel a bit tightly.

When we understand our place in the universe, we consciously create more spaciousness in our awareness throughout the day. Rather than rushing to fill periods of silence, we shift our focus away from the objective world and listen more often within. In doing so, we come to trust the boss in the back seat and learn that we can take our eyes off the road now and then.

The advice from higher consciousness can be very subtle. It doesn't always come in words or images. It may arise as a gentle wave of knowing that lifts and carries you in a new direction. It is always helpful and never asks you to do anything harmful.

Act on these nuanced nudges. You will recognize spirit's influence by the element of surprise or the burst of joy that results. When the ego aspects of our story no longer feel the need to drive solo, fear goes out the window. This is freedom.

The other night I was awakened at 3 A.M. I tossed and turned, doing my best to quiet my mind. These periods of insomnia don't happen so often that they cause concern. Sometimes they're simply the result of too much busyness during the day. At other times, spirit wants to take advantage of the early morning energy to give me a download.

As the clock clicked over to four o'clock, I sent a frustrated question to no one in particular, *Why can't I sleep?*

A subtle sensation broke through, letting me know that a gift awaited me if I got out of bed. As my feet touched the carpet, I sensed a suggestion to pick up a book that lay beside me on my nightstand. Not wanting to disturb Ty, I found it by feel and quietly slipped out of the bedroom.

Spirit spoke to me as soon as I sat in my armchair and turned on the light. In words that sounded like my own thoughts I heard, *Turn to the last page of the last chapter.*

Doing as directed, I turned to the last page and began reading. The first few paragraphs held no meaning for me, but suddenly my gaze fell upon a word that jumped out at me as if highlighted. The term *howling* was one I had used in writing the Preface to this book only two days earlier.

In the many times I've recounted that moment of seeking solace from a God I didn't yet know, I had never used that specific word. Now here it was, being used by spirit to get my attention.

As I read the rest of the page, my skin erupted in goose bumps. The next paragraph described how humans cry out to God as a method of finding our way back to our source. This cry, the author wrote, is spirit's prayer to find itself through us. I realized this was the same thought I'd had when I went to my sister-in-law's room and received comfort from God through her.

I saw now why spirit had not allowed me to go back to sleep. Joy wanted me to find this paragraph and recognize the similarities between the words I had been led to read and those I had recently written. The message was clear: I had not done so alone.

We do nothing in isolation. It only appears that way when we ride in our human vehicles and stare fixedly out at the road.

I sent a wave of gratitude to spirit and turned out the light. Sleep came easily when I crawled back into bed. I awoke at the normal time feeling refreshed and well rested. When I sat for my morning meditation, I immediately felt the presence of Joy. I used this as an opportunity to give thanks yet again for the sacred experience hours earlier . . .

"Joy, it's stunning the way you didn't let me sleep and guided me to pick up a book I'd been reading the previous day. You led me directly to words that discussed the exact subject I had written in the Preface to my new book."

It shouldn't be stunning. Don't you know by now that I wrote the words through you?

I do ask you to write through me each time I sit to work . . .

And your request is granted.

I found it interesting that in writing about an experience I've shared many times, I described a new scene and used words like *howling* that I had never written in all my years of relating that story.

You found it interesting for I was delighting in the process. I experience through you. And did I not tell you, "Fresh is best"?

You did. But to guide me directly to the word *howling* in someone else's book . . . Clearly you knew how all this would unfold.

Yes, but you almost missed your opportunity.

You mean when I was lying there looking at the clock for over an hour.

You almost didn't ask, "Why can't I sleep?" And when you finally did ask, you asked it in a generic manner instead of . . .

I get it! Instead of saying, "Hey, Spirit! Why can't I sleep?"

Yes. When you asked the question, there was barely a shimmer of asking me, but I was able to get through to you that you were meant to read something special.

I knew the feeling that something fun was unfolding the moment it arose. Before that I thought for a few minutes about getting up and doing some writing. Now I know that you put in my awareness the thought that doing so would make my mind too active, and I would be up for hours.

Correct. Once again, you thought you were doing the thinking. Be silent more often, and you will not miss inspiration from beyond.

Such an important point. Silence.

It is necessary to notice the inspiration that may not always come as word-thoughts.

I see. Inspiration may come as a vision or simply knowing what is needed.

Indeed. Now combine asking with silence, and you're golden.

Ha! Silence is golden.

If you like.

It just occurred to me that we can ask you to feed us our lines when we don't know how to handle a situation or what to say. And you just reminded me that when doing improv, actors are supposed to respond to the other actor's lines by saying, "Yes, and . . ." no matter what.

That is correct.

I see that I have fallen into the trap lately of resisting what some of the other "actors" in my story say.

This is equivalent to saying, "No, and . . ."

Thank you. I am asking you to guide me in saying, "Yes, and," and then turning to you for the best possible lines that follow.

You have noticed that your words are flowing from a higher state when you are writing.

Yes, and I thank you for these wondrous connections. Thank you for having me write, "Howling at a God I didn't know." Now I know that when Susan passed, you were right here all along as me doing the howling.

In my desire to know myself as you and through you.

But you didn't pop in at that moment when I was howling.

You were not ready to hear me as you do now. But you were desperate enough to visit me as your sister-in-law, Lynn. That was inspired.

I didn't realize that at the time.

Few do, which is why we are writing this book and encouraging people to say, "Hey, Spirit . . . I am ready to wake up!" This is a good basic phrase, but do make sure all understand that the awakening does, indeed, happen by grace. I have the bigger picture, you know. By not awakening on demand, greater things may result. Be willing to walk about blinded a bit longer, and all that you need will be revealed with divine timing. I should know.

I love when you make me laugh.

I love experiencing laughter through and as you.

I really get that. And I thank you for the miracles. Bring them on!

As you wish.

Okay, then better said, "Hey, Spirit! Bring on the miracles as they serve the greatest good."

It is my joy.

YOUR TURN

Are you ready to take your hands off the wheel now and then? The technology in many modern cars allows drivers to actually do so for brief periods when in cruise control. A prompt in the car will guide you to put your hands back in place if you stray too far outside the lines.

This is exactly how spirit will work with you using your nonphysical helpers. You can relax, knowing that Joy's got this. You only need to remain alert and actively listen as you co-create each moment. No longer will you need to run after your goals like I ran after the chairman's car.

Take this moment now and spend some time in the higher energy delivered through this latest conversation with Joy. What issue would you like help with? Is there something in your life that is causing you to say no to life instead of yes? Slow down even more and allow awareness to slide into your spiritual heart. Once in a more expanded state, ask for guidance, and await the loving directions that follow.

CHAPTER 6

ROUND AND ROUND

If you find it difficult to believe that there are other realities beyond this physical world, that's understandable. The term *reality* infers a stand-alone place or a thing that is—as the root of the word infers—*real*. Certainly the sights, sounds, and textures around us captivate our attention and give the impression of a solid world.

But is solidity the only factor in determining what is or isn't real? Most people only believe something is real if it involves a shared experience, meaning it happens to more than one person. Otherwise experiences are placed into the category of dreams, imagination, illusion, or hallucination.

Some people on the spiritual path say the world is an illusion. It is not. If you hurt your body, the pain is palpable. When you experience trauma, your suffering is very real. What is illusory is the perception of separation between physical objects. The appearance of a world "out there" is quite convincing, but it isn't the ultimate truth.

Rather than a thing existing in space and time, our universe is fundamentally an experience in awareness. It is subjective, but it seems objective because it is a shared experience within an enormously large collective field of consciousness. It operates under common constraints such as gravity and linear time, which make it seem solid and stable. From a broader perspective beyond space and time, however, all is more interconnected and fluid than it seems.

Discoveries in quantum physics have shown that at an underlying level, matter is made of energy. Particles exist in states of probability rather than fixed positions until they are observed. This observational element gives meaning to the idea of "mind over matter" and emphasizes the primacy of consciousness.

Welcome to what I call 21st Century Spirituality®, which fosters a more expanded worldview in which science and spirituality both play important roles. Science helps us navigate the objective world. Through meditation and other spiritual practices that expand consciousness beyond space and time, we experience a subjective world where the boundaries of reality dissolve.

Today, thanks to the merging of science and spirituality, more people are coming to recognize the porousness of matter and even dimensions. Synchronicities and psychic phenomena further reveal the underlying connectivity and malleability of reality. Personal experience is your best teacher, far more transformational than any written or spoken word.

Nearly everyone can relate at least one story about events they heard or witnessed that can't be explained by the laws of science. Who is the judge of whether it was real or not? What if the only "real" reality is experience itself? By this definition, anything that can be created in consciousness is real.

In my book *Wolf's Message* and the documentary of the same name, I describe a moment when the veil between the physical and nonphysical worlds parted for me personally.

It occurred when I was nudged to go to a local Barnes & Noble bookstore. I had an inner knowing that there was a book there that I was supposed to read.

I felt guided to go to the metaphysical section. I stood in front of a set of bookshelves and scanned the collection, unsure of what I was looking for, when one of the books moved half an inch to the left. I saw the movement quite clearly and heard the rustle of pages on the shelf before it moved again, back to its original position. I glanced around to see if there were any witnesses to this unprecedented experience, but I was alone in that section of the store.

When I returned my gaze to the shelves, I didn't recall which book had moved. Just as I began to question whether I had imagined the incident, the scenario repeated itself with an audible swish as the book once again moved left, then back to the right.

In that moment, I knew that I had experienced what science-minded people might call a hallucination, but it was very real to me. I also knew by then—thanks to countless experiences in expanded states—that our perceptions can be altered by higher consciousness if it serves the greater good.

As a result of this attention-getting experience, I purchased the book. It didn't take long to discover why I was meant to have it. I had recently connected across the veil with Wolf, a young man who was struck and killed by lightning like my stepdaughter, Susan. While his parents had validated much of the information he shared with me, several unusual details remained a mystery. The book I was guided to buy contained multiple photographs, drawings, and highly specific paragraphs that pertained directly to the unsolved pieces from Wolf's reading.

In metaphysics an experience such as the one where the book appeared to move is called "physical mediumship."

This is a concession to our shared agreement that the world is physical. To those who dwell in alternative realities, our world is not solid. This truth was proven to me in a similar incident that occurred several years later when I traveled to Pittsburgh, Pennsylvania, to teach a class in mediumship.

I arrived at the Sheraton hotel late on a chilly Friday night. I was scheduled to teach all day Saturday and Sunday. After settling into my room, I returned to the lobby to investigate where I might find breakfast in the morning.

Upon exiting the elevator, I spied a Starbucks coffee shop a short distance down the hallway. I approached the shop and peered through the bars of a floor-to-ceiling security gate. I made a mental note of several light breakfast items on display and decided to see if the hotel's restaurant offered a more substantial meal.

As I began to walk away, a sensation of motion from a wicker basket on the countertop caused me to stop and turn back. My gaze fell on several packets of Quaker instant oatmeal just in time to see one of them sliding downward.

I cocked my head, unsure what would have caused the packet to move. The counter was perfectly level, and no one was in the enclosed space behind the gate. As I zeroed in on the "Maple & Brown Sugar" label, the packet reversed direction and slid back up to its original position.

After the initial shock, I felt a thrill of excitement. Thanks to the incident in the bookstore, I instantly realized that a spirit was trying to get my attention.

Okay, I said silently, *who did that?*

I sensed no one around me, but I heard a very distinct giggle.

Just then a short, attractive woman with eyes as dark as her hair came around the corner, walking toward the elevator. Seeing me, she stopped and broke into a broad smile.

Identifying the common look of recognition from a stranger who knows me, I said, "You must be in my class this weekend."

"Yes," the woman replied. She introduced herself as Kim Milano and expressed her eagerness to learn how to connect with her loved ones in spirit.

I wondered if a family member of Kim's might have been responsible for the incident with the oatmeal. Not sensing a clear presence, I chose not to mention it. We exchanged a few more pleasantries, then said good night. Kim continued to the elevator, and I went to check out the restaurant's breakfast menu. On the way back to my room, I took several photos of the Starbucks shop and the basket filled with oatmeal packets to document the unusual experience.

The energy in class the next day was high, as kindred spirits on both sides of the veil gathered to learn how to communicate with each other. Halfway through the morning, I gave the class a break. I wandered to the product table where a line formed with students who wanted me to sign my books. I recognized Kim Milano when she arrived at the front of the line.

Following a hunch, I asked Kim if there was anyone special she had hoped to connect with that weekend. She nodded vigorously.

"Oh, definitely! My mother."

I shifted my focus to the spirit world, but I still could not sense the presence of anyone in Kim's soul family. Still, the timing of seeing the oatmeal packet move moments before Kim approached me the night before felt significant.

"By any chance," I said, "did your mother like oatmeal?"

Kim gasped so loudly that everyone within earshot stopped whatever they were doing and turned to look at us.

Many people like oatmeal, but Kim's reaction was so exaggerated that I knew I had zeroed in on what I call a "gold nugget." These are details about a person's life that stand out in a way that differentiate one spirit from another.

My questioning look prompted Kim to explain, "She liked oatmeal so much that she ate it every night!"

"Every night?" I asked, appreciating that the timing and regularity of her mother's indulgence took oatmeal beyond a generic breakfast meal.

"Yes!" she confirmed with visible excitement.

"And I have a feeling that maple brown sugar was a favorite flavor," I said, connecting the dots even more.

"Yes again!" Kim said now, clasping her hands to her heart. "In fact, maple brown sugar oatmeal was the last meal she had before she passed."

My skin erupted in truth shivers as I motioned Kim to the side. I quietly explained how her mother miraculously manipulated matter the night before to get my attention. When I asked if I could share this wondrous experience with the class, Kim willingly agreed.

When class started after the break, I began with a discussion of how malleable reality is. I used this fresh example of physical mediumship to amplify the lesson. As I publicly thanked Kim for allowing us to honor her mother's efforts, Kim raised her hand. "May I tell you something?" she asked.

"Of course."

She stood and addressed the whole class. "My mother loved being the center of attention. She would be thrilled that you're making a big deal about her now in front of everyone."

The class laughed as I corrected Kim. "Your mother *is* thrilled because she's right here soaking up all this love." I realized then why her mother had held back energetically, only allowing a giggle to slip out the night before, so that we could celebrate together. "She's having fun sharing the excitement with all of us now," I said, "and letting you know she is still very much a part of your life."

To this day, I affectionately refer to Kim Milano as "Oatmeal Kim." I keep a packet of Quaker Maple & Brown Sugar oatmeal across the room from the desk where I do my readings. It serves as an ongoing reminder of the miracles that those in spirit are capable of pulling off when it serves a higher purpose.

Life is often likened to a dream, especially when we experience events that defy our common explanations. When we awaken from a particularly intense dream, we say, "It seemed so real!" And it was real—as an experience within the mind.

In lucid dreaming, the dreamer is aware of being half-asleep. As we awaken to our true nature and realize that all that exists is the dance of consciousness at different levels of reality, we become lucid.

Human perception is not limited to normal waking consciousness. Instead, life unfolds along a spectrum that includes dream states, meditative states, and even altered states. The latter can occur as the result of spiritual or somatic practices or from the use of mind-altering substances.

No matter the cause, each of these states allows us to transcend the familiar and enter a world of limitless possibilities. Doing so leads to heightened clarity, creativity, and a greater understanding of how we fit into the grand scheme of being.

I recall driving through the town of Fruitland Park, Florida, quite a few years ago, when suddenly everything in my line of sight became pixelated. People strolling along the sidewalk took on slightly robotic movements, giving the impression that I was watching a video game.

I had not been daydreaming. On the contrary, I felt hyper-aware of my surroundings and sensed that I was being given a brief glimpse at just how illusory our world truly is.

The boundaries of physicality dissolved for me yet again while hiking the Sulphur Mountain Trail in Banff National Park in Canada. Ty and I usually enjoy the outdoors in silence. On this occasion I decided to listen to the ethereal music of Deva Premal through headphones as we climbed.

The trail snaked upward beneath a cable car carrying less intrepid tourists to the summit. We had only been hiking for a few minutes when the ground beneath my boots began to undulate in gentle waves.

I said nothing to Ty about what I was experiencing. I simply observed this unexpected phenomenon with curiosity as it continued. Normally I would breathe heavily from the exertion of climbing steadily up such a steep trail. Instead I flowed rather than hiked with a sense of awe as the music carried me effortlessly upward through 33 switchbacks.

When we reached the top after ascending more than 2,000 feet over three and a half miles, I knew that I had gone through some kind of time and space warp. My heart rate and breathing remained slow and steady. I felt euphoric, aware that there was no physical explanation for what I had accomplished.

"Let's do it again!" I shouted to Ty only half jokingly as I held my hands to the sky. By grace I had been given a glimpse of heaven, where the limits of the physical body do not factor into our experiences.

This is not meant to downplay the importance and beauty of our human bodies. They are perfectly designed for the soul's adventures on Earth. Even the body's malfunctions serve as opportunities for growth and learning.

Other dimensions remain largely obscured to the physical senses. This is by design. If the brain's filters suddenly opened, removing the illusion of separation for all of humanity at the same time, the game would be over.

But that's not going to happen anytime soon. Birth and death follow a cyclical, winding path like the Sulphur Mountain Trail, carrying us ever onward, ever upward as part of the evolutionary trajectory of spirit.

Planet Earth is a school for the soul, where we come together not as a punishment but to create and play with consciousness as the clay. Here we dance and sing with our classmates, joining in at different stages in each other's journey, much like singing a round. Who can forget the children's song "Row, Row, Row Your Boat" and the joy of hearing the harmony that naturally arises as voices interweave?

Yes, life is but a dream. And with each go-around, we become ever more lucid. And we find ourselves back where we started, having come full circle, remembering that in reality there really is no separation between us. Together we form one indivisible whole singing the one song of our indivisible uni-verse.

Pause for a moment, if you will. Take a calming breath, and slide awareness from the head to the heart. From this expanded state, feel the words in the conversation with spirit that follows as you read them . . .

A CONVERSATION WITH JOY

Joy, I have been connecting across the veil since 2009. I interact every day with guides and loved ones who have passed. I have had enough "no other explanation" moments to share for days, and yet when I'm doing things that are not related to mediumship or meditating, there are still times when I have to convince myself that the greater reality is real. I put meaningful reminders around the house to help me remain lucid, but why is this even necessary? Why do I live what sometimes feels like a double life?

Because you are walking about IN the dream.

You mean this physical world?

Merrily, merrily, merrily . . .

Ah, Sanaya recently said, "Just lift your oars and float." Now you're saying, "Merrily, merrily, merrily," as in "Row, Row, Row Your Boat."

Yes, the writer of that ditty knew truth.

Wow. Your answer as to why I can't maintain awareness of the greater reality is so obvious . . . and powerful. We are immersed in the dream . . . caught up in it as we walk about in it.

Did you not one day hike for over a mile of rocky desert terrain without watching your feet or the ground before you? You had surrendered.

That was an interesting experiment. I wanted to see if I could be guided every step of the way.

It took what?

Cooperation.

And what else?

Great presence and attention.

Yes. People say you "leave your body" when you experience altered states of consciousness, but there is nowhere to go. Awareness simply focuses on two realities at once. To refer to such experiences as alternative realities is more accurate than saying "two worlds," for there is only one world, but both phrases are meaningful.

So if we could learn to walk in two worlds at once, holding the awareness that this is not the only reality as we walk about in it . . .

This would be mastery.

I am not there yet.

You may not want to be.

Why not?

For you came here to dream.

Wow. That has a very cool double-entendre feel to it.

Yes, we are here to dream in the sense of creating something wondrous. And what could be more wondrous than to become aware that you and everyone else in the dream share the same source?

Here we go again.

That is what I said when I began dreaming.

How many times can I say "wow"?

Now you understand my motive in dreaming.

Now I understand why I had that experience of seeing everything pixelated like a video game and how I have seen physical things appear to move.

It is good that you used the word appear. *All is simply appearing in awareness. Nothing is really out there. That is the greatest realization you can come to if you want to truly become lucid.*

Ah, there's that word, *lucid*. That's the key, isn't it? In lucid dreaming we are aware that we are dreaming, but we keep the dream going.

And how much control do you have over the dream in that case?

Only a bit more. Just a bit.

Exactly. And yet you seek to control this dream, when it is our dream.

Hmmm. I notice that you didn't say, "It is my dream."

That would be accurate, but not completely so, for you are having this conversation within the dream, making me into we.

We've come back once again to our interconnectedness. And yet the pull of the dream is so strong that most of us kick and scream when we realize how little control we have.

This is what happens when ego gets lost in the dream. I am not lost. I am enjoying life through you.

And that's the bottom line, isn't it? We get upset when someone calls this a dream because it's very real to us. People get hurt. People die. There is real suffering.

Only when you lose awareness of truth. Whether you call it a dream, a reality, a world, or simply the ongoing experience in awareness that life is, it is all "love in full expression."

I would like to remain more lucid in this LIFE.

You awaken more fully while doing the readings and when talking to me as you are now. Hold on to this awareness in between.

But now you're showing me that because I have not been fully awake within the dream, we are having this conversation now. You want me to share this with others. This feels like when Susan came to me and explained why she did not reveal her presence from across the veil for three long years of my daily efforts to connect with her. She deliberately held back.

And did you not expand your abilities and your awareness greatly in those three years?

Very much so. And looking back I'm grateful, but at the time, it was frustrating.

And did you not feel frustration as you began this conversation, asking, "Why can I not remain lucid at all times?"

I was being used again?

Perhaps.

I don't know whether to laugh or cry. May I remain lucid now?

Are you sure you want to?

That's the thing. Now I'm not sure I want to. It's really fun to get excited when the miracles happen.

Which is why surrender is such an excellent practice. Leave the awakening to me. Allow me to become lucid as you and through you when the timing is right. There are certain experiences yet to come when you will want to dive in fully to the human experience.

Should I be afraid? Wait. I know that is a silly question. I have nothing to fear. I have enough lucidity these days to know that my body will react with fear when necessary to protect me, but then lucidity kicks in, and I can shift to soul awareness.

Which is when you turn to me.

Yes! So, knowing you are always here to guide me, I can simply get back in the boat now and row gently. Wow. Okay. I know this is a dream—an experience in awareness from a specific state of consciousness. It is one very real dream, but I'm here for the ride.

Well done. There will be other analogies to help you remain lucid. For now, trust the stream.

I can't thank you enough. I'll try not to put myself down anymore for getting caught up in the dream. I will trust that if and when I am meant to be lucid, I will be lucid. You will pull me out of the dream, because you are the ultimate lucid one having one experience with all of us in it.

Quite merrily so, dear one.

YOUR TURN

What concepts introduced in this chapter caused you to squirm? Use this time to dialogue with spirit and uncover the reasons why you may not be singing in harmony with the uni-verse. There is no need to change anything immediately if you feel resistance. Just relax, lift your oars and flow . . .

CHAPTER 7

BEST-LAID PLANS

The first six chapters of this book practically wrote themselves in six exhilarating weeks of nonstop inspiration. I experienced almost daily the kind of connection I hope to inspire you to establish with spirit. And then, several weeks ago, the conversations with Joy stopped. The inspiration dried up. I sat at my keyboard a few times during that dry spell, but no amount of trying produced anything readable.

I know what writer's block is, and I can tell you that the flow wasn't blocked. I had simply been put on hold, and I knew it.

I am sharing these events with you to demonstrate how you, too, can accomplish big and small tasks with far greater ease when you come to realize you need not do anything alone. Incredible freedom results from trusting that you are always connected and that higher consciousness will guide you moment by moment when you attune with it. What may seem like an obstacle in your path is often an indicator that there is a better way to achieve your goals or somewhere else you need to place your attention.

Prior to signing the contract to write this book, my attention was undeniably focused elsewhere. I had agreed to lead seven two-hour modules of spiritual teaching for an Awakened Way cruise to the Caribbean. I promised the participants different material from past at-sea workshops, knowing that spirit would provide new teaching and insights. The trip was less than three months away, but I set that deadline aside when the first few chapters of this book started bubbling up.

Each time I sensed the slightest concern about my need to prepare for the at-sea retreat, I turned within and received the same response: *Work on the book. All is in perfect order.*

And indeed it was.

The day I finished Chapter 6, I was guided to open the cruise folder on my laptop. For the past few months, I had been saving random notes from spirit that I knew were meant for the workshop. Now, just as easily as the first chapters came together, the various "Awakened Connection" modules fell into place. I saw the overall plan as if spirit had revealed the cover of a puzzle box in my mind's eye.

I thought that perhaps I could work on the cruise program and write the book at the same time. I continued to sit in meditation each morning while working on the retreat modules. I received the daily message from my guides, Sanaya, yet no amount of wishing could conjure up the uniquely magnetic and mesmerizing energy of my special dialogues with Joy. I knew I was being asked to have faith in the journey and set that writing aside.

And so, with the book deadline always held dimly in awareness, I let it go. And then yesterday morning, the unmistakable "pick up your iPad" feeling came when I closed my eyes to meditate. The wave of energy brought a burst of joy, and I typed my initial greeting to that welcome voice.

The words that followed let me know that the conversation was destined for this book, but I found myself wondering if the next chapter would flow as easily as previous ones had. After such a long dry spell, I could only trust.

My schedule for the rest of the day did not allow me to do any writing. I didn't worry. I had learned that if I was meant to work on the book, the time to do so would open up naturally without me having to rearrange anything.

I slept well that night, but I awoke earlier than usual. Unable to get back to sleep, I slipped out of bed at 5 A.M. The feeling that nudged me toward my laptop carried a wordless yet unmistakable message: It was time to get back to the book. I realized then that spirit knew my schedule better than I did. The next two hours would be the only uninterrupted time in the day ahead that I would have for writing.

Still in my bathrobe, I turned on the light in my study, sat at my desk, and opened File Explorer. I had no idea how long it had been since I had last accessed the book files. It was far longer than my human side would have been comfortable with in the past. I was the kind of student who always completed my assignments well ahead of a due date. I never would have put off a task based on inner guidance like I do now.

As if wanting me to know that I had done well in trusting the process, a message arose in awareness. I was shown that if I checked the date when I had last accessed the book's files, I would see divine perfection in the timing.

With the familiar energetic signature of a gift unfolding from spirit, I noted the date on the most recent file and compared it with my online calendar. My spirit-driven sabbatical had lasted so long that I had to expand from "week view" to "month view." Seeing how the dates aligned, I broke into a smile.

It was precisely four weeks to the day since I had worked on the book. Had I accessed the file even five hours earlier, the synchronicity would not have been as meaningful.

Due to such a long respite, I had forgotten what I last wrote. Spirit guided me to spend a few minutes reviewing the latest pages, so I opened the file marked "Round and Round." It didn't take long to see that the previous day's conversation with Joy had picked up the thread beautifully by mentioning *Wolf's Message* in both the sixth chapter and in the new dialogue meant for Chapter 7.

As I further reviewed the topics covered, Kim Milano's name stood out. I had not seen her since the workshop in Pittsburgh four years earlier when her mother so cleverly moved the packet of oatmeal.

I only recently agreed to host a screening of the *Wolf's Message* documentary near Kim's home. I now saw yet another timely God-wink in the fact that after the long period of no contact, she and I had met face-to-face in a Zoom meeting the day before.

Are you beginning to see how all things connect? Do you understand that you and I are points of light—patterns of energy and information—in a vast field of indivisible consciousness? When you start to notice these patterns and connect the dots, you will experience your own God-winks more often.

And so, the flow continues now effortlessly as I write these words. It wasn't a case of writer's block. It was a matter of allowing spirit to set my priorities for me.

As Wolf came back to teach us from across the veil, we are part of one big web connecting all that is. Knowing this explains why in the midst of putting together the modules for a 14-hour cruise workshop and writing a full-length book, I agreed to take on a third major project: a tour that would take *Wolf's Message* not just to Pennsylvania, but to 30 cities across the United States.

Planning such an undertaking is no small feat. Yet when Ty suggested the idea to me with a starting date only two months away, I could only laugh and say, "Why not?"

Some people might say I'm an overachiever or possibly even a little crazy. Both might have an element of truth. But in all honesty, I have come to trust spirit so thoroughly that I knew we would have all the earthly help we need and that spirit would guide us unerringly. Truly, when you learn to turn within, the inner guidance is so precise that it will tell you which task to work on at what time and for how long.

And indeed all the details of the tour are falling into place with as much ease as the other two projects. It is a joyous experience for all involved, for we know we are part of something much greater than our individual selves. Godwinks abound, revealing help not just from guides, but from the loved ones in spirit of many of those involved in the film.

Instead of feeling stressed out or calling any of this "work," we are flowing as a team and growing ever stronger in our trust. Like the patterns of energy you will read about in the fresh conversation that follows, we are not spiraling out of control while handling our earthly assignments. On the contrary! We are experiencing firsthand the evidence of our interconnectedness. It is pure Joy, and it is available to you as well when you turn within and trust.

Good morning, Joy. You just guided me to play the video for the *Wolf's Message* documentary and slide the bar until you said to stop. I intuitively sensed that it would stop at an important message, and that's exactly what happened.

Do tell.

Ha! Clearly you want me to tell! So, it started playing right where I'm on-screen talking about how Wolf knew it's all about the oneness. I described how he got this message across by showing me patterns of shapes such as triangles, spirals, and circles.

What does oneness *mean to you?*

Funny you should ask me that, because I learned about it from you!

And what have you learned?

That beyond the appearance of physicality, everything is patterns of energy vibrating in one field of energy and information. That one field is the root of the oneness, meaning that everything is always connected, like threads in a tapestry.

More than you know.

Why can't I know more?

Because you are seeing the field like a snapshot or, to use your analogy, like a tapestry with a fixed image sewn into it, when in fact the field is dynamic beyond your imagining. It contains images within images—infinite connections eternally arising and dissolving.

But once connected always connected, right?

Go back to the oneness. I said "dissolving" not "disconnecting." You cannot be disconnected from the field energy. You exist because of the field energy. You are the wave.

Like the analogy of the ocean and the waves that can't be separated from it.

Yes, but remain with the "field of energy-information" analogy, for it is closer to what is going on. The "waves in the ocean" analogy conveys the true sense of connectedness, but it lacks the sense of purpose that underlies existence. Waves in an ocean simply undulate, but waves in a field of energy-information carry meaning that can be comprehended. Where there is meaning and understanding, there is evolution.

Wow. There's another memorable phrase, like "Intention plus action equals experience"!

You have a good memory, little wave.

Ha again! It's not my memory, is it? It's simply you, the field, activating the precise pattern of energy-information contained in that phrase at a higher level than little me, yet I call it "my mind" and "my memory."

You're catching on.

At your whim, because I'm really starting to understand how few of my thoughts are my own.

How can they be, dear one, when all arises from the one?

From you?

Who am I who speaks to you now? Not the entirety of the field. You could not receive such a high-frequency transmission. It would blow out your circuits, so to speak.

I'm picturing—or better said, images are arising now in awareness of the vastness of our galaxy.

It is one of billions of galaxies. And if each of the hundred million stars in a galaxy were one thought, do you think the thinker of those billions upon billions of thoughts would communicate to you like this in such a simple manner?

It boggles the mind.

Exactly. Boggling is not helpful when the goal is evolution.

Hmm. So, I want to know who's speaking now, and I suppose it doesn't matter, because it's obviously a higher level than the pattern I refer to as "my mind," and it is helping me understand the one mind.

Yes, the field itself is the one mind.

So, these patterns that Wolf showed me—the triangles, and the spirals, and the circles . . .

Wordless ways of sharing energy-information and the underlying fabric of reality in a manner that crosses culture and language.

Everyone understands circles. The wedding band is such an excellent example of union and completion.

Yes, it represents the wholeness which you already are as a pattern unto yourself within a field that represents the one true self.

But I and all of us in human form are not closed circles. We're more like spirals, ever evolving, ever growing. You've shown me that.

Correct. The spiral is a most excellent image to hold in awareness when you feel you have no purpose. You arise from the field as the expression of Joy that you are, and onward and upward you go, ever expanding as you grow.

And we continue to vibrate as patterns of energy-information—to experience our stories—at your whim?

Not a whim, dear one. Pure Joy. It is impossible to hold all this potential without bursting forth.

As us.

Indeed. Shine on, for that is what the light does.

The light of Awareness. You are the one light that becomes us to shine on your behalf. So beautiful.

As I have said many times: It is good, no matter what. And as you so precisely had me say in the movie when speaking for you: You are perfect as you are, for you are already divine.

YOUR TURN

Would you like to experience greater flow and less stress in your life? I hope I have demonstrated in this chapter that such a goal is possible. First, set the intention to align with spirit as often as you can remember to do so. Second, surrender your need to plan everything to the smallest detail. (Trust me: As a former quintessential list maker who used to facilitate strategic planning sessions, if I can live surrendered to spirit, so can you!)

After you've shared your intention with spirit, get in the habit of pausing before you make or consult a to-do list. Instead, say, "Hey, Spirit! What's the best thing for me to act on right now?" And then simply listen. Notice what arises. If what you sense is helpful, follow the guidance.

Does this make you a puppet on a string? Not at all! Once you see that turning to spirit is like having the best executive assistant on the planet, you may do as I do and say, "Go ahead, Spirit, pull my strings!"

CHAPTER 8

WHAT IS REAL?

What a blessing it is that our world is populated with visionaries. The new technology and inventions we enjoy are gifts from those who imagine possibilities and turn them into reality. If someone had told me when I was a child that one day I would have a portable, wireless telephone small enough to fit in my pocket, I don't know if I would have believed them.

And if they had told me that I could casually call out, "Hey, Siri!" to that phone and instantly access answers from something vaster than the encyclopedias in our family's living room, I would think they'd been watching too many episodes of *The Jetsons.*

It is those who are willing to think outside the box who advance humanity. The fact that you have read this far shows that you are open to stretching and possibly even upgrading your BS for the sake of your soul's evolution. The willingness to be flexible when it comes to trying new ideas and practices on your spiritual path can lead you to unexpected but mind-expanding adventures in consciousness.

One of my most memorable adventures happened in 2013. In my efforts to fine-tune my connection with spirit, I gathered weekly with a circle of friends to channel my guides, Sanaya. In mid-December, Sanaya advised us to do a special meditation on Christmas Day. They alluded to a special gift awaiting those who did so.

I don't know what gifts the others received, but following Sanaya's guidance, I entered an expanded state of consciousness early that Christmas morning and received far more than I expected.

Once I was fully relaxed yet alert, I asked to have an encounter with any master who could help me on my journey. I had no expectations as to who would show up. I sat quietly and simply watched the sensations, thoughts, and feelings that arose in awareness. After only a short while of noticing and allowing the random ST-F in my mind to come and go, I became aware of a powerful masculine presence.

In the sessions I do for clients, I rarely see the spirits' faces. This day, however, I clearly saw a grizzled old man with long white hair. He looked very much like depictions I had seen of Moses, but I intuitively sensed this was someone else.

I engaged him with a greeting and mentally asked, *Who are you?*

A single name arose in awareness: *Odin.*

I vaguely remembered hearing someone in the history books called Odin. I couldn't place the name in any meaningful context, however.

Tell me about yourself, I requested with an implicit request for evidence.

The response came in a mix of clairaudience, clairvoyance, and clairsentience. The spirit replied, *Odin comes to teach you the secret of the runes. There is much wisdom there.* Next he showed me the image of a horse with wings. This was followed by a piercing sensation that caused me to yelp and grab my left side just below the rib cage.

As I noted these details on my notepad, Odin added, *See the rune shaped like a lightning bolt. It has great meaning for you.*

Certainly lightning was meaningful to me. My stepdaughter Susan had been killed by lighting as was Wolf, the young man whose story I told in my book and in the documentary *Wolf's Message.*

Is there a rune with a lightning bolt? I questioned. I had learned about runes—a set of 26 stones with symbols that are used as a divination tool—from Wolf, who dropped in on me from the spirit world and told me to pull a rune. When I did as Wolf requested and pulled my very first rune, I "randomly" drew one that directly related to a story involving a wolf.

What do you think? Is there one or not? Odin replied with no hint of humor.

I hadn't studied runes at the time, but now I made a note to look for the one he mentioned.

I felt Odin withdraw, and I brought myself back to normal waking consciousness. I immediately headed for my laptop and googled "Odin." I was not happy to read that he was a mythological figure considered the All-father of the Norse gods. How was it possible that I had just engaged in a two-way conversation with someone who wasn't real?

I searched my memory but could not recall ever having studied Scandinavian mythology. I would have immediately dismissed the experience were it not for the image next to his name. The drawing showed the exact likeness of the man I had seen with long white hair and a beard. I was further intrigued by the two wolves at his side.

I scrolled down the page and learned to my astonishment that the story of Odin included an eight-legged flying horse named Sleipner. Equally eye-opening was an epic poem attributed to Odin that included two more validations of this bizarre visit. The famous poem told the story of Odin hanging for nine days and nights from the tree of life, pierced in the side by a spear precisely where I had felt a pain so tangible that I cried aloud.

According to legend, Odin gained wisdom from stones on the ground while hanging upside down. These stones became known as runes. A quick image search for the word *rune* showed that indeed there is a rune shaped like a lightning bolt. It portends transformation, power, and spiritual growth—topics that were certainly meaningful for me, as Odin suggested.

By this time in my experiences with expanded states of consciousness, I had accepted the existence of guides and angels. I knew of no one in my growing community of spiritual seekers, however, who claimed to have spoken to a mythological figure. My beliefs were being stretched to their limit.

I could have spent more time seeking answers online, but I chose to honor the very real experience that had unfolded subjectively. I returned to my meditation room and used my time-tested BLESS ME Method* to once again align my energy field with higher dimensional frequencies.

Like switching the channel on a remote control, my intention accessed the nonphysical dimensions, and I invited Odin's return. When I felt the familiar lightheadedness of another being's energy field merging with my own, I silently inquired, *Odin, are you here?*

Yes.

---

* I walk you through this practice in Chapter 3, and you can learn much more about it in my book *The Awakened Way.*

I noted the distinctively powerful personality I had felt earlier and got straight to my most pressing concern: *You were allegedly a powerful god, but were you real?*

He replied, *As real as you are, but not human.*

I increased my will to overcome the doubts that threatened to break this connection. With all the power I could muster to maintain a high vibration, I protested, *But you are a myth!*

Key indicators that you are not making up the thoughts that arise in meditative states are that the information perceived is spontaneous, fresh, creative, and not what your ordinary human mind would consider. Odin's response filled each of these requirements when he instantly retorted, *YOU are a myth!*

I did a mental double take as I processed this unexpected statement. *What did he mean by claiming I am a myth?! How dare he accuse me of not being real!*

Until that point, no spirit had ever shared anything with me that was less than kind and loving. Odin's words seemed to diminish the value of human life.

I quickly realized, however, that he hadn't said I wasn't real. He said I was as real as he was. And what is a myth after all? Myths are stories . . . experiences woven together into a seamless narrative that provides meaning to events and serves a purpose. Isn't that what we do with the memorable moments of our lives?

For years I have been teaching others that we are souls experiencing life through our individual stories . . . our myths. Still, as I considered Odin's surprise declaration, I fidgeted. The presence of this alleged Norse god with a flying horse escorted by wolves was definitely making me uncomfortable. He wasn't unkind, simply firm and authoritative.

Reverend Temple Hayes, the former pastor of Unity Church of Tampa, once counseled me that if I wasn't causing my students to squirm a bit, then I wasn't doing my job. Hadn't I asked for a master in spirit to assist me on my journey? And here was a historical figure named Odin who was doing his job quite well, causing me to seriously question my beliefs about reality.

He continued to do so now, asking, *Can you appreciate that I am not a standard teacher from one of your books? Your rational mind would have made excuses that you already knew the details of my existence and are imagining this interaction. Open your mind. I am consciousness, as are you. Listen and learn.*

I did listen, and what he said next became a quote that I would commit to memory. I share it often in my teaching these days. It is one of the most important concepts that we in our human roles can grasp about ourselves and the nature of reality. Odin said:

You must stop differentiating between real and unreal. Do you not know now that angels and gods and archetypes are real? Anything that you can create in consciousness is real and can convey truth, messages, information, learning, healing, and growth. All is not as it seems.

At the time that Odin shared this wisdom with me, I had connected with thousands of beings across the veil. Our connections had allowed me—just as Odin stated—to convey truth, messages, and information that the spirits' family members validated. The information gleaned from these very real experiences most definitely provided learning, healing, and growth.

Odin's visit allowed me to see that we too often view things as either true or false, real or unreal. This "either/or" human perspective is very limiting. Quantum physics operates within a broader structure that recognizes things can be *both* true *and* false at the same time.

Was Odin real? Yes and no. From the human perspective, he is not solid. If perceiving something through the physical senses makes something real, then he would be considered unreal. But most people, when questioned, will admit to perceiving and knowing things without having to touch, see, smell, or hear them. Our inner experiences are very real to us, as Odin's visit was to me.

Humans tend to give greater credence to a story or label something real if it is a shared experience. The more people buy into something, the more "real" it becomes. Yet who can deny that dreams are very real to the dreamer? The fact that no one else had the same experience does not take away from the learning and insights that can result from a powerful dream.

When it comes to determining whether an experience is real, personal experience and point of view are paramount. From the perspective of nonmaterial beings and humans who have experienced communication with those in the nonphysical realms, the spirit world is real. From the perspective of source, the material world and what we call the spirit world is neither real nor unreal. It is all simply consciousness.

The 13th-century Sufi poet Rumi didn't question the reality of his connection with the Beloved. His words dripped with trust. I thank spirit for nudging my friend and spiritual teacher Scott Taylor to send me this poem by Rumi just now as I write about perspective and reality. Read it slowly and truly digest his great wisdom:

Pay no attention to what the gossips say.
They call the wide-eyed flower jasmine.
They call the wide-eyed flower a thorn.
The wide-eyed flower doesn't care what they call us.
I adore that freedom. I bow to it.

Some say you worship fire.
Some say you follow scripture.
What do they know?
Labels blind and tear us apart.

Your eyes are not a vulture's beak.
See through the Beloved's eyes.
See one when your mind says two.
The angels adore your [Be]Love[d]-drunk eyes.

Open them and dismiss the vicious judge
from the post you gave him.
*Bow to a human and greet the angel.**

After his initial visits, Odin dissolved back into the field of energy-information. And then three months later, he appeared unexpectedly in my morning meditation. Before I could greet him or ask him where he'd been, he surprised me with a blunt and mysterious question:

Who was my son?

Caught off guard, I thought for a moment, and then I recalled the Internet search I did when Odin first appeared to me. I smiled, knowing I would pass his pop quiz. *Your son was Thor!* I announced like a proud student.

Yes, he replied solemnly. *And what was the name of your stepdaughter's dog?*

I pictured the very last photo we had taken of Susan before she passed. She was lying on her couch, curled

* Rumi, *Gold*, trans. Haleh Liza Gafori (New York Review of Books, 2022). Bracketed text is mine.

around her brand-new puppy. When I searched my memory and remembered the dog's name, my eyes flew open. I rudely broke my connection with Odin, rose from the chair, and rushed from the study. I found my husband standing at the bathroom sink brushing his teeth.

"Ty!" I said so sharply that I startled him. "I just had another visit from Odin, and he asked me what Susan's dog's name was. Remember the puppy she got just before she died?"

He rinsed his mouth and looked at me thoughtfully for a moment before replying, "I remember the dog, but I don't recall its name."

"It was Thor!" I said excitedly. "The same as Odin's son, and Thor is the Norse god of thunder and lightning!"

It took a moment for the significance of these synchronicities to sink in. Then Ty's eyes widened to match mine. I don't know what startled us more: the awareness that our Susan had chosen Thor's name three months before being struck and killed by lightning or the fact that the All-father of the Norse gods had dropped in to help us connect the two events.

In that moment a thought arose from beyond my conscious mind. "Wait a minute," I said, squinting. "There's something else . . . What was Susan's other dog's name?"

"I don't remember that either."

Trying is counterproductive when accessing memories. Thoughts and images from the past are not stored in our brains. They exist for all eternity in the one shared mind. So, standing in the bathroom, I closed my eyes and asked the universe, "What was Susan's other dog's name?" And then I let the question go.

I turned to leave the bathroom. I took no more than three steps toward the door when the answer bubbled up effortlessly into my awareness. I whipped around and said, "Oh my God, Ty, her other dog was Loki!"

He gave me a puzzled look. He wasn't as familiar with Odin's story as I was.

"Loki was Odin's adopted son! Both of Susan's dogs had a direct connection to Odin!"

It would be years before we would recall that Thor was the third dog in Susan's household and Loki the second. The first was a female mixed breed who Susan had named Athena. The stories of Athena in Greek mythology are legend. She was the daughter of Zeus, the god of lightning that Sophy Burnham referenced when she brought Susan through to us in our very first reading.

When I realized that Susan had given each of her three dogs a name with a connection to either Odin or lightning, I sat in meditation and asked her to come and talk with me. She answered the call, allowing me to feel her lively, loving energy.

I greeted her with a wave of love and then got right to my most pressing question, *Just like Wolf, your soul must have known that you would be killed by lightning, didn't it?*

I didn't know it consciously, she replied. *I was too focused on my life with my new husband and the baby we were expecting. But the soul is always as close as your breath.*

I know, I said, thinking how much my understanding of reality had expanded as a result of her passing.

I was basking in the welcome feeling of Susan's presence when something thoroughly unexpected happened. Suddenly, like watching a science fiction film, Susan's image in my mind's eye morphed into Odin's. Exactly where I had sensed Susan on my right side, I now saw and felt the grizzled old teacher with the white beard.

I shook my head in an effort to understand what had just happened. Before I could ask him, Odin morphed back into Susan.

I felt a moment of dismay. Had Susan been playing with me during Odin's previous visits? Was she disguised as him? Odin had none of Susan's energy. He didn't look like her or speak like her. Had I been duped?

I knew that Susan wouldn't play with me like that. I wondered if I had experienced what some people call a trickster spirit. If so, I could never share this with anyone publicly. They would think the spirit world isn't real. I was truly squirming now.

And then Susan, who remained in my awareness, put everything into perspective for this story known as Suzanne: *It's all malleable,* she informed me.

You said you wanted to experience oneness. We're all one, Suzanne! Your guides are here, and Jesus, and Archangel Michael, because there's only "here" in the one field of Consciousness. We are all the same, just different instruments in one symphony! Which instrument you focus on is the one you experience. You as Joy can play any of these roles, because it's all God, and the more you surrender, the greater the connection and the power.

My human side wanted to know if Susan was Odin. My soul, said, *Throw off the shackles and flow with the possibilities.*

Reliving the experience of feeling Susan's energy one moment and Odin's very real presence the next, I realized the truth in her words. We change our roles all the time within our families, in the workplace, and in every interaction we have with others.

The very malleability of consciousness also allows us to step out of our roles as actors on the stage of this "either/or" life where we try to fit experience into boxes labeled "real" or "unreal." It affords us the gift of being able to rise onto the balcony where we become observers of our stories and flow with greater ease as the drama unfolds below.

I had turned within and said, *Hey, Spirit, bring me a master.* In so doing, I took the lid off a suffocating box and stepped into a world that is far less stifling and palpably steeped in love. It didn't matter if I called my visitors Susan or Odin. Joy had appeared in one of its limitless roles with a powerful demonstration that "*all is not as it seems.*"

Who is it you would like to connect with? What is it you want to know?

Do you wish to have a conversation with a loved one who has passed? You can't do that on the Internet. Do you want to hear what they have to say to you when you reach out? You won't find that by asking Siri.

Do you wish to find clarity, comfort, and direction when you feel lost, alone, and confused? You find these by listening to the spirit within.

You (yes, you!) and all other beings, including your loved ones who have passed, guides, angels, and the masters are all aspects of consciousness. Because spirit is indivisible, you can use this eternal, indivisible bond to make a personal connection with any of its limitless creations as it serves you and the greater good.

Is it real when your heart expands to overflowing from a knowing that you are not alone? Is it your imagination when you sense a presence and hear advice that helps you better navigate life's challenges? If the words *real* and *unreal* did not exist, would you simply trust your heart? What would you then *know* when you turn within to make a sacred connection?

Follow your heart. Like Rumi, you may just bow to the Beloved who speaks with and without words if you will only reach out and engage.

Joy, what do you say to those who think they are making up their connections when they sense a loved one who has passed or any other spirit being? Are these connections real?

Susan coming to you was real and a figment of consciousness.

I love that expression! I am feeling the human fear of people dismissing spirit communication if we use the word *figment*.

Fear is simply an indicator of where you need to shine the light of awareness. Embrace your fears. Cause others to squirm a bit. Be a fearless explorer. You have told the Odin story in the past, but you have hesitated to tell that he and Susan morphed into each other. To share this without fully explaining that nothing is real and everything is real could cause confusion. Now others will come to understand that all this is a figment of consciousness. Does it make it any less real? How real are your dreams? They are also figments of consciousness.

I get this. And some might say that these adventures in consciousness are imagination.

And what is imagination? Imagination is consciousness dancing and playing. That is how new insights and growth occur. If you only base decisions on what has already happened and what you consider real, you get nowhere. Are you ready to leap?

Yes, with the highest possible guidance.

Then be not afraid and use your unseen assistants. Take the leap.

So it's not a case of either real or unreal.

I prefer "both/and." You and Susan are both real and figments of consciousness, as are all the beings you commune with. Does this mean you no longer attempt to speak to figments of consciousness? Of course not. Such conversations are real. Ask instead, "Does it serve the current story to connect with higher consciousness?" If so, then do attempt to speak to these figments and hold the intention that doing so furthers the story. If done for reasons that only serve the figment, then what is the point? You only become more lost.

Are there trickster spirits as some people claim?

The question that matters is, "Are these conversations helpful and healing, and do they lead to growth and evolution?" All are figments of consciousness. All are, as the name of your guides, Sanaya, implies, "One worth knowing." It is one and the same, just as Odin told you: You are just another part of me.

It is all story, whether you call it The Story of Suzanne or The Story of Susan, or any name or label you may choose to use. How else can I, Awareness, express myself other than through moments knitted together in meaningful ways to form a narrative?

That's key, isn't it?

Yes, meaningful. This is a most important detail. What is the point unless meaning is here? And so, I arise and speak with you in my many forms. Yes, this is "me" speaking to "you," and in this relationship, "I" finds meaning. Now perhaps you understand how "I" needs "you." Without "you," LIFE has no meaning.

I get it.

Without "you," I AM no-thing. I have no meaning. There is no sadness in this. I enjoy simply being, and I also enjoy arising and interacting. The cycles of being-doing-being-doing are for the Joy of it. Onward we shall go with you in greater awareness of who Joy and all my stories have been all along: Formless and formed. Nameless and named. Now you know I am your self.

What is a good practice to continue integrating this awareness that is so clear when in an expanded state yet disappears when we return to our human stories?

Hold the focus, hold the focus, hold the focus on present moment awareness. Scan the full sphere of awareness, noticing what arises. Be curious about what would have been missed had ego distracted you. Stay in the upper floors of consciousness yet fully aware of the body through presence, so that you can judge what state you are in.

Thank you. What aspect of you is talking to me now?

Your imagination.

Oh my God, you are so very funny. You feel like Sanaya right now.

One worth knowing. I AM here now to give you your daily message to share far and wide with other aspects of me.

Thank you so much.

It is my Joy . . . Here you go:

Go there in your dreams . . . that place where magic happens . . . where anything is possible. Go there in your daydreams without dismissing them as folly . . . that state where ideas spring up and dance with each other. Go there in your waking consciousness . . . that childlike state of imagination, play, and wonder, and wonder no longer just how much is possible for you. Take off the shackles of the rational mind that hold you prisoner to thinking. True creativity arises from beyond the brain that you have learned to revere so much. Whether you call your experiences dreams, daydreams, or "real life," it is all LIFE: love in full expression.

You are so very loved. It can be no other way.

YOUR TURN

One of the most common questions people ask spiritual teachers is, "What is my purpose?" Spirit tells us that we as souls came here to create and evolve. As anyone who has ever built or created something new knows, all tasks are made much easier and produce far better results when you use the best tools.

Your most powerful God-given tool is consciousness. Your thoughts, visions, ideas, and choices manifest your reality.

I have done my best in Part I to help you to understand that you are inseparable from the field of consciousness from which all that exists arises. When you fall into the trap of thinking you are separate and that you have to handle everything alone, life is more difficult than it has to be. I hope that even if you have difficulty embracing your innate divinity, you are by now at least willing to play a bit with your creative superpower and aim to have your own adventures in consciousness.

I am reminded of a conversation I once read in which a woman allegedly asked Thomas Edison, "Sir, what exactly is electricity?" Edison is said to have replied, "Madame, electricity IS. Use it."

Scientists have since helped us understand electricity, but they, like spiritual teachers, philosophers, and laymen, are still challenged to agree on what consciousness is. To me the definition isn't as important as realizing what expanded states of this omnipresent, omnipotent, creative, intelligent force can do to help bring more peace, joy, and love into our moment-by-moment experiences.

To that end, I like to paraphrase that statement attributed to Thomas Edison and say, "Consciousness IS. Use it."

In Part II, you have a chance to do exactly that as a way of finding answers and insights into some of the most challenging universal issues we as humans face.

Today we have Siri and artificial intelligence to help us when we need guidance. But these are secondhand sources. One of the main goals of this book is to get you in the habit of instinctively turning within for the most deeply satisfying answers and an unmistakable sense of connection that is your birthright.

This next section gives you the opportunity to practice that habit and access higher consciousness yourself. It also provides the possibility to greatly expand your consciousness, for not only do the channeled essays in Part II contain deep spiritual wisdom, they also carry the higher vibration of spirit. As you read the words, your own field will naturally rise to align with these frequencies. You may wish to come back and read them again and again.

Turn the page now, and embark with me on a journey to access Spirit directly. The methods I introduce will allow you to be both passive and active, attuning to and integrating with the universal wisdom that your soul already possesses.

PART II

INSIGHTS FROM WITHIN

INTRODUCTION TO PART II

With the advent of artificial intelligence (AI), we can now instantly find answers to our most pressing questions and concerns. The information we obtain from an online query can be satisfying and helpful, yet there is a critical element missing from AI: It has no *direct* connection with the spiritual heart that connects us to each other and to all of creation.

Yes, everything that exists arises from the one field of consciousness, so technically even "artificially" acquired information is a derivative of our shared source. But the artificial part means that it is at least one step removed from the divine intelligence and love that flow through and inform each present moment.

This is where relying on and listening to higher consciousness as your first go-to for guidance rather than turning outward to objective sources truly returns the best results. In this section we will explore 25 common human issues and challenges with a focus on obtaining insights that come as close to being direct from higher consciousness as humanly possible.

To kick off the introduction to this section, I was guided to choose a subject from a list of topics I had compiled for the book. I was drawn to the words *Understanding and embracing forgiveness.* Using my BLESS ME Method, which I detailed in Part I, I entered a state of expanded awareness and asked spirit to share the highest possible wisdom about forgiveness.

I immediately sensed spirit in the form of my guides, Sanaya. Their words flowed far easier than these are now, demonstrating the difference between passively listening to spirit from a whole-brain state and actively writing from only a left-brained perspective.

Sanaya began their discussion as they often do, with a clever turn of phrase, making an important point about our place in the world. Next they addressed me personally by saying, *Hear us well,* a phrase they often use when they want to emphasize what follows.

I then recognized them referencing a poem about forgiveness that I channeled from spirit well over a decade ago. I recalled the approximate time period, because this was early in my spiritual awakening when a group who called themselves "The Council of Poets" dictated without pause a fresh, creative poem to me each day in meditation for just over a year. Knowing that I had never been one to write poetry, spirit used this clever way to help me know that I wasn't making up my connection with these higher beings.

The Council trained me in listening and trusting their presence until turning over the reins on the morning of my birthday in 2010. After receiving the 369th poem, I felt a powerful presence with both masculine and feminine qualities. When I engaged them and asked who these new spirits were, they told me they are a collective consciousness of guides and that I would write and write as their channel. And indeed I have served as both their scribe and their voice—almost exclusively in prose—since that initial gathering.

For our purposes here, I asked for an essay. Their words about embracing forgiveness flowed as a two-way conversation. As you will discover as you read the essays that follow, Sanaya always engages us directly, ensuring that we experience ourselves *embraced* by their powerful yet loving energy. In this case they paused twice to directly ask, *Do you see?*

I share these details as examples of how to tell when words you sense from listening within are flowing from consciousness beyond your personal field. Were they directly from your personal individuated consciousness, they would not have this kind of interactive, conversational feel.

When I returned to normal waking consciousness after receiving the initial download about forgiveness, I read the words and felt a flush of pleasure at the free-flowing method my guides had chosen for this section of the book. It's always easier to turn tasks over to spirit, and with over a decade of channeling Sanaya, they were making this easy on me.

I sensed, however, that I would not be able to force the process. Even though I had a very human deadline from my publisher, I would not be able to produce spirit's words on demand. I surrendered and trusted that spirit would deliver all that was needed according to their own timeless schedule.

Now it was time to compare the difference between saying, "Hey, Siri!" and "Hey, Spirit!" The guides wanted me to compare the essay they had just given me with an essay about forgiveness derived from AI.

Thanks to a group of spiritually minded tech geniuses at an organization called Awakin AI and my assistants Meredith Ortiz and Jayesh Mitha, we harnessed the power of artificial intelligence to create a section on my website called "Find Answers."* Here visitors can instantly access the immense treasury of teaching amassed from Sanaya and the poets since 2010 along with transcripts from all my spiritual books, classes, podcasts, videos, and webinars.

There has been a bit of fear surrounding the use of AI, but the guides showed me that AI is a blessing when used with the intention of serving the higher good. I now saw the opportunity to compare the freshly channeled essay on forgiveness with one derived from the "Ask Suzanne and Sanaya" feature on the "Find Answers" page of my website.

With this as the plan, imagine my surprise when I reviewed the contract for this book and found a clause prohibiting the use of AI while writing it! Certainly this is a reasonable request that reflects the times in which we live. Any original work should be derived solely from the author's own creative inspiration, but this new requirement put in question the method I was shown by spirit to use.

I wrote to my editor and explained that I wanted to use AI to prove the premise of the book: that turning directly to spirit is the optimal choice when seeking comfort, clarity, and direction. Happily the publishers agreed to reword the contract to reflect the specific purpose that I disclosed.

With this approval I went to the "Find Answers" page on my website. It displays four ways to access spiritual wisdom. The first is a static list of the most frequently asked questions from followers of my work. A carryover from my original site, the answers came the old-fashioned way—with

---

* "Find Answers," Suzanne Giesemann, https://suzannegiesemann.com/find-answers/.

my assistant Bev Garlipp combing through the archives of channeling sessions with Sanaya long before we ever heard the term *artificial intelligence.*

The second resource allows visitors to instantly search the hundreds of videos I have recorded on my YouTube channel using relevant keywords. This amazing technology returns a list of every video in which the keyword is used with a link to its precise location in the video. A search for "forgiveness" brought up nine pages of results with 84 distinct links.

The third method searches the archives of over 6,000 of Sanaya's daily messages by specific search terms, returning the top five most relevant responses. Each of the spirit communications that came up in response to "forgiveness" was beautiful and insightful but provided only one short paragraph of prose.

Hoping for an equivalently lengthy response to the channeled essay received earlier in meditation, I selected the fourth feature, "Ask Suzanne and Sanaya."* In the search box I wrote, "Please give me an essay from Sanaya on understanding and embracing forgiveness." Like most search engines, only seconds passed between clicking Enter and seeing the results unfold on my screen.

Having tried the AI function during our initial beta testing, I knew the answer would be appropriate and helpful. I did not expect it to have an element of surprise that revealed the hand of spirit at work. Of all the ways it could have responded to my prompt, it focused upon one of the poems that I received from the Council of Poets in November 2009. Out of 369 poems received that first year that I connected with spirit and thousands of pages of transcripts

---

* "Meet Grace: The Awakened Way Companion," Suzanne Giesemann, www.SuzanneGiesemann.com/yourquestionsanswered.

of my work, the supposedly "artificial" intelligence chose the same poem that Sanaya brought up in their channeled essay for this book.

The "Ask Suzanne and Sanaya" feature is programmed to end each query with Sanaya's familiar phrase, "You are so very loved," so it is no surprise that both essays closed with these words, but it is clear that both the direct and indirect methods are derived from the same source.

Poem #132 about forgiveness was far from my conscious mind when I sat and queried my beloved guides in the here and now. By referencing the same poem in their spontaneous channeled essay before it arose from AI, we can celebrate how spirit provides exactly what we need to show us the web that connects us, be that the World Wide Web or the cosmic web of consciousness.

Sensing energy is a subjective endeavor. I found the AI version a bit less satisfying than the more interactive experience that resulted when I took the time to enter an expanded state of awareness. While using AI is faster and easier than turning within for wisdom, the words received using human technology have a more sterile vibration.

In meditation, as I described above, Sanaya revealed their innate cleverness, using creative word choices and vibrant, visual analogies to impart their teaching. The tone is conversational and engaging; the content is fresh. In other words, the direct method of obtaining information is more personal than using modern technology.

Most meaningful to me, I had the personal experience of interacting with wise teachers. I felt their care for me, their companionship, and their love. That is my goal for you as you enjoy and experience Part II of this book.

When my friend and assistant Patty Hart, who you met in Part I, read and compared the AI and meditation versions, she grew quite excited. Here is what she shared with me afterward:

> On my walk this morning, I purposely didn't bring my phone to listen to music because I wanted to think about these essays and marinate in the energy a little bit more. The experience made me think about lyrics to a song and how—until they are put to music with melody, harmony, and beautiful instruments—they are just words. They come to life with the music!
>
> When we go to AI for information, we get words that come with definitions, but we don't necessarily get the deeper meaning. The AI version lacks emotion, and sensitivity, and energy, and color . . . just like in music!
>
> It's similar to texting. When someone sends you a text message, you don't actually hear the tone in their voice or the emotion that their words hold. You see and read the words, but often there is a miscommunication because the receiver of the text reads and interprets the words differently than the sender intended. They can't hear the voice and the energy behind those words.
>
> When Sanaya speaks through you, there is an energy and a vibration and soulfulness that makes all the difference in the world! It's like seeing a black-and-white picture, and then all of a sudden, the color arrives, and it changes the whole perspective of what you're seeing. Colors and melody

and harmony carry beautiful vibrations that bring words to LIFE!

This is the distinction I hope that you will experience as you go beyond simply reading the insights I received from spirit in the pages that follow. I wish for you to turn inward and receive your own download from spirit. I want the words you receive during your inner journeys to feel nothing less than *intimate*.

I initially thought that I would provide an AI version and a meditative essay for each of the 25 issues chosen for this section. The initial exercise with forgiveness as the topic showed that this is unnecessary. You only need to do the comparison once to realize the benefits of going directly to spirit.

Therefore the following pages contain channeled essays that I received in my direct communications with higher consciousness. While I know you will gain insights from reading them and will be tangibly uplifted by the higher energy they transmit, that is not their sole purpose. They have a soul purpose as well. They provide a point of comparison for words that you are encouraged to obtain from your soul's perspective while in an expanded state.

The goal is for you to learn to trust that you are never alone and that insights and higher guidance are always available to you. Whether you are new to this type of practice or an old hand at turning within, I recommend you use the following method to hone your discernment:

- Read the essay title and contemplate your current beliefs about it. Notice if the issue raises any less-than-positive emotions or causes your body to tense. If so, be curious rather than judgmental about why you're experiencing constriction. Examine more closely your personal assumptions about the topic.

- Read the channeled words provided. Notice what thoughts and feelings arise as you do so. If you feel resistance as you read, be curious as to the cause. Is there something about this topic that you have particularly strong feelings about? Is there anything you could ask spirit to help you understand more deeply?
- Say, "Hey, Spirit!" (or whatever feels natural and comfortable to you) and request your own insights on the issue. Relax as fully as possible and directly ask some aspect of higher consciousness to teach you in depth. Be silent and observe what arises in awareness. Write down whatever you perceive.
- Once you return to normal waking consciousness, compare the insights you received with the ones in this book. Are they similar? Are they helpful?
- Contrast your previous perceptions about the issue with what you learned from spirit in your meditation.
- Acknowledge what you have gained from doing this inner work and send a wave of gratitude to spirit.

An alternative method from the one above is to read the essay title and see what information you discern from within *before* reviewing the channeled words provided. Doing so will help you learn to trust and rely first and foremost on your own connection to spirit.

Be aware that the goal is not for you to come up with insights that match my channeled words. The purpose of working in this way is for you to connect with spirit yourself, discerning fresh information and guidance about these issues that you might not otherwise have considered. The practice may bring surprises as you tap into wisdom that comes from beyond your conscious mind. Trust the words when they speak to your heart.

And now, when you are ready, dive into the topics that follow. By doing so in the manner proposed, you will be learning to live the Awakened Way . . . consciously connected always to your own inner guidance and aware that you are divinely guided at all times.

Understanding and Embracing Forgiveness

Why in the world would you want to "embrace" forgiveness when most people hear the word and wish to run in the opposite direction? For you are in this world, but not of it.

Hear us well: When forgiveness becomes an issue, there is hurt for all those involved, which includes the one asking for forgiveness and the one giving it.

Forgiveness, as we have stated in a poem well over a decade ago, doesn't come with power or might. It doesn't speak of wrong or right. It is a tool that takes energy that has become misaligned with the soul's patterns of harmony and realigns it so that all are in resonance. It allows one to operate once again in a state of coherence.

Where there is incoherence, forward movement is stalled. Where there is harmony, dancing can once again take place.

Embracing forgiveness means going from a state of restriction and lack of forward movement to freedom of flow. This is what the soul knows. The soul knows how to dance without stepping on toes.

The soul adores freedom, which is why it lets you know in no uncertain terms that something must change when hurts, judgments, and lack of understanding keep one trapped in a holding pattern.

If you could see how those caught in blame and shame appear to us, you would be quick to forgive or to ask for forgiveness. There are energetic bonds holding the two dancers as if there is a cord between them. There is no coming or going. There is a stuckness.

To forgive someone is not equivalent to saying, "You were right, and I was wrong." It is energetically akin to saying, "I have been seeing you as separate from me. I know that this situation would not exist if we had been aware of the dance of our souls. Now that I see we are both souls and humans, I wish to allow the soul to determine how I move about the floor. I wish for freedom for all, and thus I forgive myself and I forgive you for ever thinking we are anything less than love."

Do you see? It is not about the story. In stories there is always a "me" and a "you," an "us" and a "them." And where there is this division, there will be hurts and anger and blaming and shaming. When you shift to the soul's perspective, you see such attitudes weighing down your movements like those selfsame dancers wearing heavy boots. It is nigh unto impossible to dance like this, beautiful soul.

Thus the only forgiveness that is ever needed is forgiving the forgetting of who you really are. The moment you blink back into awareness that you are all souls dancing your way through the challenges of life, forgiveness comes naturally.

Now you are free to make choices within the story about that which led to this "dis-cording." Such choices, we dare say, will be based now on love, which arises quite naturally from the awareness that ultimately there is no separation between anything or anyone at all.

With this awareness, you now want nothing more than to embrace each other at the soul level and perhaps even with the body. And this you can do now freely from the heart, which is no longer bound to a temporary story.

And so, do you see? It matters not who is right and who is wrong. Those are elements of a story. In the human story, there will always be darkness and light. One day it is you, and one day it is them asking for or granting forgiveness. The dance goes on.

Embrace the duality, but do so from the soul's perspective where right and wrong are reconciled with awareness of I AM. All else is story.

If forgiveness is difficult, you are still trapped in the story. It is that simple.

You are so very loved.

❁ ❁ ❁

Here is the original poem on forgiveness received from the Council of Poets in November 28, 2009:

SPIRIT POEM #132

Forgiveness—
The greatest gift . . .
When used to heal a painful rift.

Those who harbor pain and anger—
Who hold for others hardened rancor,
Hold within their chest a stone
Leaving them to feel alone.

Yet when you find it in your heart
To heal that which does set you apart,
Then you know the inner peace
That enters with a great release.

It comes when you can finally say,
"I do forgive you on this day."

It doesn't carry power and might.
It's nothing but a touch of grace
That brushes softly 'cross the face.

And without judgment says, "I know
That all of us are here to grow.
And if I send you love, not hate,
Then easier will be your fate."

For all must pay for what they do.
You face your actions, this is true.
But seeing that we all do err
And showing that the love's still there
Then in this way you show to all
That even those who take a fall
Can walk the straight and narrow path
When met with love instead of wrath.

A prompt for your own experience

Enter an expanded state of consciousness. Invite a higher being to merge with you and ask, "Spirit, please give me a new perspective on forgiveness and show me how to apply this in my life here and now."

Hope in Times of Despair

Are there not times when you have cried out, "I cannot stand this!" and all you wish to do is collapse into a heap? We understand this, for your suffering is very real in these moments when the truest part of you becomes so clouded over with what is in your here-now of awareness that you lose all sight of the blue sky of awareness.

Despair is a feeling that you identify with the loss of hope. You are convinced, however temporarily, that things will never change.

How to dig yourself out of this well of despair? Stop digging, dear one. Pause. Perhaps even allow yourself to lie in the heap of thoughts that have brought you down. And in between your sobs and wracking breaths, you may just notice a point of no sobs and a state of no breath.

These gaps between the misery have a quality all their own. They are not filled with the thoughts and sensations that have dragged you down. Instead there is a lightness. In what may feel like a state or place of nothingness, there is actually a fullness. There is potential here in these gaps . . . the possibility of something different from what you are caught up in.

And that space, that gap, that emptiness that is actually fullness is the birthplace of hope, if you will only notice. This is the center point that is always present. It is present between all action. It is the being side of doing. And it is where you meet your self coming and going.

Now reach out or call out. It matters not how you access this endless source of assistance, but in the reaching or in the calling—and you may call it what you want, but we prefer the term prayer—the part of you that knows despair is acknowledging that something else is there . . . a state or place of being that truly does care.

That "certain something" that arises from the gaps in doing—in the space between despair—is the source of hope. There is a part of you that remains aware, no matter what, that all will be well. There is a part of you that remains aware, no matter what, that you are not alone.

There is a part of you that knows beyond any doubt that underneath the surface woes, the universe is good, and you are a part of it. Knowing this at a level you may not even be able to identify is what gives you hope, what encourages you to cry out, and what energetically strokes your cheek when you feel you cannot lift a finger.

Hope is God's gift that keeps you seeking something more than despair. Hope is the possibility in each moment. Hope is the light in the darkness. It is a very real thing that arises from the state of no-thingness. In calling out, "Oh, God, give me strength!" you have acknowledged hope.

Just as peace lies always here within, so does hope. These are innate qualities of the soul—that aspect of your wholeness that often gets set aside as you roll about in the muck and mire of being human. Fall down or rise up. Both are very human actions. In the "being" state of being both human and a soul is where you find hope.

You are so very loved.

A prompt for your own experience

Enter an expanded state of consciousness. Invite a higher being to merge with you and ask, "Spirit, what do I need to know about hope?"

Giving and Receiving Love and Compassion

You have heard, perhaps, that to give love, you must know love. Do you not yet understand that you are this love? It is not a thing. It is your very essence.

In your experience, love comes and goes in waves. This is because love is the inbreath and outbreath of the state of pure being. "What is pure being?" you ask. Pause for a moment, if you will, and notice what is in the pause.

There, for the briefest of moments, you experience complete and utter silence, complete and utter peace. And yet within what seems like nothing is everything, for you know from experience that in a moment, a thought or some other sensory input will arise. These are the waves of being. They flow. They arise from and subside back into pure being. You cannot separate them from pure being. They are its arising and subsiding.

This, dear one, is flow. This activity of pure being is part and parcel of its existence. It is all connected. And what does this have to do with love? Why, everything!

This all-pervasive presence of being cannot stay still for long. It must rise up and extend itself, and in so doing, it experiences itself as something that appears other than itself. And yet because the waves are of itself, it knows only connection. This is love. To know that all experiences flow as one from one source is to know love.

But this is not the human version of love that fills your heart with a burst of joy that leads to longing for more. This filling and bursting are gifts that cause you to stop looking outward and focus on the source of this feeling, which you will acknowledge as the heart. In other words, the burst of chemicals that results in a feeling you call love is a guidepost to turn inward and know the connection that will lead you home. You cannot be cut off from this source, for you are the very outbreath and inbreath of being.

Now do you remember?

And so, now you have a natural urge to give love—the breathing out aspect of being. And you receive love, which is akin to breathing in, and on and on it goes, this flow of being, giving, and receiving your very essence.

The challenges arise when you get caught up in the foam on the waves from the sea of love . . . the countless bubbles of thoughts, images, and sensations that remove attention from the basic rhythm of breathing. But here is the good news: When you cease looking outward and turn inward with the breath, then, in this momentary cessation of fixation on bubbles, will the awareness bubble up: I am love.

This is a by-product of your very being as the undivided wholeness of being and flowing. And if you are love, and there is no separation between you and the source of the outbreath of God that you are, then what of those around you? The animals, the insects, the birds, and the beings you call people are also the outbreath of God. Therefore all are "love in full expression."

Do you know this definition of LIFE? You are that, as is all that you experience, dear one. And knowing that you are both an individual expression of love and the fullness of love at a deeper level, you cannot help but feel compassion for those who suffer. And why do they suffer? For they are focusing on the bubbles instead of the waves of love and how they flow.

If you wish to give and receive love, find a mantra that reminds you to keep your focus on the flow of LIFE. Slowly, slowly, you will come back into harmony with your true nature and compassion will be the norm. It can be no other way when you remember.

You are so very loved.

A prompt for your own experience

Set aside time to go as deep as you can in a meditative state. Ask for higher consciousness to inspire you with the difference between human love and divine love.

Cultivating Patience

You will notice in the chosen title that the goal is cultivating patience. This gives the idea of something that is first an idea, then from this a seed is planted, then the seed is nurtured and given the proper environment and nutrients in which to grow, blossom, and bloom.

Can you wait for the present moment to unfold? Why, you have no choice. And what if you have no preconceived idea of how this moment will unfold? Why, then you simply are present and observe with curiosity what is unfolding, what is present . . . how reality is showing up.

And if you have a preconceived idea of some ideal now-moment, now what? If it comes to pass, you are satisfied. And if it does not come to pass as you envision, you are dissatisfied. If there is a remote possibility that satisfaction lies in waiting, then there is a sense akin to a clock ticking. And in that tick-tick-ticking, you may develop a tic, for there is now another sense added to the mix of sensations . . . that of incompletion.

Did you know that satisfaction is very fleeting? It is quite different from contentment. The latter lingers. The former comes and goes like the wind that blows leaves hither and thither. Patience is like that. It comes and goes dependent upon whether you are aware of the underlying contentment or blown about by the vagaries of satisfaction.

And what underlies it all? The thoughts to which you choose to give your attention. Patience or lack thereof depends upon whether those thoughts pertain to the present moment and all that is so beautifully arising in the present sensorial moment or whether the thoughts are focused upon some not yet realized future.

Ah yes, impatience is cultivated in a thought rooted in a not-yet-realized event. Patience arises quite naturally from the awareness that beneath the breeze is a consistent inbreath and outbreath of being. As you learn to trust this breath to carry you inexorably onward and upward just as the sun pulls a plant's stalk upward with no impatience whatsoever, you begin to relax.

This may seem like a bit of bluster to make a very simple point: Patience arises from presence and trust. Impatience is the by-product of allowing the mind to wander into a not-yet-realized future.

How to cultivate presence? Lovingly plant the seed of intention to remain present and trust the flow of being. Water this intention and give it plenty of sunlight in the form of your trust that what you think must occur now now now is not as critical as what is actually occurring now now now.

Observe the blossoming of patience as you observe what is here now now now, and we dare say patience will bloom quite beautifully in your life in ways previously unimagined.

You are so very loved.

A prompt for your own experience

You may think you know all you need to know about patience. Empty the mind and relax as fully as possible. Knowing that a wise being will hear you, ask from the heart, "Please show me what I need to know about patience and how I can cultivate it in my present circumstances."

Managing Anger Constructively

Do you realize that emotions are indicators? They are not beings you must obey, yet they can feel this way, for emotions are very much rooted in the body. They push and tug at you, causing you to want to act.

Anger is a most powerful emotion. For some it can be frightening. You may wish to run away when faced with another's anger. Perhaps you react the same way when anger wells up inside of you, feeling the imminent loss of control should you express the full force of what you are experiencing.

And herein lies the clue to managing anger. You will note that we did not say "controlling anger." Circling back to our first words, emotions are indicators. You would not want to control a traffic light. You trust that the light indicates what you are to do and that this is in your best interest.

If you were to go when the light indicates that you are to stop, you would eventually find yourself in a dangerous situation. Likewise, you do not want to control—as in stop—any emotion, least of all the most powerful ones. You wish to acknowledge the indicator and, just like with a traffic light, use discernment in that moment of noticing what color is the emotion. Is it red, yellow, or green? Do you stop, change course with caution, or move ahead with purpose?

And so, you can set the intention to pause when you notice anger in the mind or body that you might normally automatically react to. Having paused, you can determine if there is cause for action. You can now choose wisely how to react instead of being impulsive.

This is management. This is acknowledging the physical body and how it is programmed to keep you safe. And it is also acknowledging that the same mechanisms that attempt to keep you safe also tend to block your inner knowing. At the deepest level, there is no duality of emotions. It is from this level that solutions to that which causes anger and angst will arise when you pause for discernment.

"Why am I angry?" you may ask when you feel a yellow light of caution. "And if I act on this indicator, what will be the consequences?"

Anger is often a sign that you sense an injustice that may need to be addressed. Anger can also indicate that you are perceiving a wrong that may or may not need correcting. Many perceptions are rooted in your belief systems. And so, you may wish to ask, in this moment of discerning anger, if others are as angry as you are. If not, then perhaps you might use your innate gift of curiosity to wonder why you are angry and others are not.

Should you not receive an answer to this wondering, then acknowledge help from on high and ask those at higher frequencies if there is a different way to perceive that which is causing you anger. Could there be beliefs that it would behoove you to modify so as to find greater peace? Could it be that you are trying to do too much, and your anger is actually impatience? Could it be that you have noticed another's behavior, and your anger is actually jealousy or judgment? Could it be that something has reminded you of what you want but no longer have, and your anger is masking sadness or grief?

Do you see? In not controlling or pushing away anger, this indicator that something requests attention may turn out to be a blessing. If you instantly push away anger in a controlling manner, you may miss the gift it brings you. If you stuff down the gift of anger, you are missing an indicator that something is out of balance.

Do you see how it helps to reframe patterns of thinking and acting that perhaps no longer serve you? Anger is not a foe or a friend. It is an indicator with no meaning of its own. Only by noticing anger and being inquisitive do you discover the specific cause of this powerful emotion in each instance of its arising. Now you are becoming a master of the waves of emotions instead of being swamped by them. Now perhaps you will not lash out in anger the next time the light turns red, but stop, look both ways, and proceed as guided.

You are so very loved.

A prompt for your own experience

Take the time to relax completely and shift your focus to your soul's perspective. Invite a higher being to merge with you. Ask, "Spirit, please share with me insights about anger that will help me on my journey."

Comfort and Healing After Loss

When you contemplate the concept of comfort and healing, perhaps you think of turning to another like a mother who will hold you and smooth your hair, touch your face, or hold your hand. Touch is comforting for the sense of connection it evokes. And it is this very sense of touch that is missing when one you love has transitioned from the body. For this reason, you call one's death a "loss."

This is a most fitting example of the "both/and" nature of reality when one's perspective is rooted in the physical world for a while. From the physical perspective, indeed, the loss of one's presence is quite real. You feel this absence like a physical pain. At the deeper levels, what appears physical is also an energetic experience within the mind, but it does not help to hear this when one is grieving. The experience is very real, and when the energetic patterns of a loved one are no longer swirling about in awareness, suffering ensues.

How to find comfort? By creating new energetic patterns based on the awareness that your loved one is not lost in the energetic sense. This is the "and" portion of "both physical and nonphysical" in energetic terms. You and your loved one who has passed are both souls for all eternity. A soul is a unique pattern of energy that is recognizable and identifiable. You give this pattern a first and last name when you recognize the pattern in physical form. We are here to tell you that the pattern continues, and the name goes with it.

If this sounds impersonal to call your loved one a field of energy when what you long for more than anything in the world is to see and touch and interact with them again, then understand that you must simply shift to an alternative way of seeing and touching and interacting.

"How can I touch one who is no longer in a body?" you may ask, and this is where you must think outside of the body. Can you picture a bird in the mind's eye here and now? Yes. As you read these words, you are picturing said bird.

Can you hear the words I love you, in the mind's ear? Yes, just reading the words you hear them. Can you imagine the feel of a warm blanket coming out of a dryer? Yes, the mere thought of such a delight invites the same reaction of pleasure in awareness. None of these experiences are physical, yet all of them are actual events energetically, for each carries the energetic signature of the concept behind it.

Now extend this concept to one you love with all your heart and soul and invite them to draw near. Listen for their messages with your mind's ear. Search for them in your soul's sight. Feel them burst forth in your heart. Arouse the touch of their hand on yours. In so doing, all these sensations are very real. In so doing, you are keeping active in awareness the very presence of your loved one's frequency.

Is it just a memory? Not always. And herein lies the difference between imagination and experience: As you create the loved one's thought patterns in awareness, they are called forth from the one mind to dance and play. This mind is quite conscious, aware, and intelligent. It is this one mind that has breathed you into existence and does so in a physical body as you read these words. Understand that this same mind breathes your loved one into existence as you call upon them.

This one mind is breathing all experience. This one mind is the one heart of connection. Ultimately there is only one soul from which you and your loved ones arise. It is for this reason that love never dies.

May you find comfort in this awareness. May you find alternative ways of being as you navigate the ever-changing patterns of love in full expression. May your suffering lessen as you release your grip on the past and dance with Joy in the present, knowing you are both a human who grieves and a soul who breathes beyond the body.

You are so very loved.

A prompt for your own experience

Set aside time to meditate on the topic of healing from loss. Don't just think about it; shift your attention away from the thinking brain to the heart and ask, "Spirit, what is a new and more helpful way to me to understand and reframe the concept of "loss"?

Discovering Life's Purpose

You will notice the title of this discussion. It does not say, "Here Is Your Life's Purpose," for where would be the fun in that? Why did you play hide-and-seek as a child? For there is a bit of fun in knowing some treasure is out there waiting for you, and it is up to you to find it. If it were out in the open, where is the joy of anticipation? Where are the bursts of excitement at finding clues along the way?

Do you see? You are playing hide-and-seek with your life's purpose. Oh, yes, it is the same for all of you, and we will get to that shortly, but your unique life's purpose has been hidden just enough to allow you to feel a bit of frustration. And what is frustration? If you read the previous essays, you know that emotions and feelings are indicators. Frustration is an indicator that something is on the horizon, like the sun rising, but for now all you see is a bit of a glow.

There is a glow within you that has been there since your first breath. It is from the spark that never dies, the light that never goes out. This is essence . . . your inner beingness. And just as in the game of hide-and-seek, it is your task to find that spark and to keep digging, digging, digging.

What happens when you dig? You pull away the dirt that obscures the hidden treasure. And that is what you are doing as you seek the light within: pulling away the layers of dense energy that have obscured the beautiful light that you are, dear soul.

Along the way, in this search for the hidden treasure, the joy builds in anticipation (for the soul knows the game all along).

Your human side becomes more and more in touch with your true nature as the soul who willingly hid the light.

You, the soul, knew that taking on the mantle of a body would be enough of a veil to allow the game to begin with your first incursion into the human reality. And oh my, was there not a moment when you took in that first breath and then let out a big wail as if to say, "What was I thinking?!" And those around you, standing behind their veils, rejoiced at your cries, reminded by the miracle of birth that the game is still on.

And so as both the player and observer of the game, now you have a subplot: to find your individual purpose. If the larger purpose is to reveal the light of the soul within, then your individual purpose is to see in what direction you will shine.

What ignites your soul when you focus the light of your attention on a certain activity? What attracts you repeatedly, giving you a lift as you dive in and use your God-given gift of creativity to create sensations, thoughts, and feelings that align with the soul?

Perhaps you never thought of soul alignment. It occurs as you do or say something that makes you feel so good inside that you simply have to do it again. Perhaps you did not realize you were aligning with your true nature when you did something that caused another joy, relief, or pleasure. Could there be a hint here as to your purpose?

The soul already knows it came here to shine. The soul knows that given your body, your circumstances, and the abilities that are uniquely yours in this lifetime, you have the opportunity to use these in service to the whole. Now it is simply up to you to shine your light in that direction.

If you have not yet discovered this purpose that is uniquely yours, why, simply ask yourself in what way(s) are you unique? In what ways do you shine? What activity truly lights your fire and makes you want to light up those around you?

The answer may or may not stroke the ego. Do not concern yourself with strokes for now. The more you dig away the layers of human nature and reveal your hitherto hidden treasure, the more ego will simply fade into the background as you shine your light brilliantly in all directions.

There is great Joy in the discovery process. So for now, dear one, game on!

You are so very loved.

A prompt for your own experience

Enter a relaxed and expanded state of consciousness. Shift awareness beyond your story and ask whoever has the highest answer for you, "Spirit, show me what I as a soul came here specifically in this lifetime to do."

Practicing Gratitude

You have heard so many techniques for raising your vibration. Which one works the best? Perhaps you already know the answer: It is gratitude.

Why is this so? Gratitude takes you beyond the self. In expressing gratitude, you are acknowledging that you are not handling all your challenges alone. With gratitude you are saying, "I had help with this, and therefore I can look forward to help whenever I need it."

Gratitude is a thing, an experience, a state of mind, and a feeling. As you think of someone or something for which you are grateful, notice where you feel gratitude. You move from thinking in the head, and awareness slips into the heart area—the seat of the soul. Gratitude links you with the soul—your ever-present state of being that often becomes obscured by worry and busyness.

Gratitude takes you beyond the lower vibrations that are part and parcel of being human. It offers a reprieve for as long as you can maintain this state of appreciation. Is appreciation the same as gratitude? Not exactly. With appreciation, there is a bit of separation between you and that which you are grateful for. You appreciate as an observer.

With gratitude, you are all in. Roll around in gratitude, for this vibration of acknowledging your innate interconnectedness with the flow of life lifts you to a higher state. Now you can appreciate. Now you have gone from victim or experiencer to observer. Thank you, gratitude.

Our title here refers to practicing gratitude, and indeed you will want to make it a practice to consciously feel and express thankfulness. "There is always something to be grateful for" is an eternal truth. Make a promise to your higher self that you will consciously seek the blessings in your life regularly.

Perhaps you will want to set a reminder until doing this practice becomes a way of life. We dare say the more you practice this practice, the more you will have to be grateful for. And that is how it works. Gratitude begets gratitude. And is that not something to add to your list?

You are so very loved.

A prompt for your own experience

Ask spirit to show you ways to bring more awareness of gratitude into your life. Set the intention of reviewing the things for which you are grateful at least once a day until this becomes a sacred ritual.

The Illusion of Perfection

Who ever said you had to be perfect? Perhaps it was the images you saw from those trying to sell you something. Perhaps it was one who has known great success, and you mistakenly believed they are perfect, and you must be like them to find success for yourself.

Do you see how the ego works? It is very happy to hold you trapped in a pattern of seeking an elusive state of no flaws and no mistakes.

Do you not yet understand that you came here to experience the fullness of LIFE? The only aspect of life that is perfect is the wholeness of being itself. Once you as source arose and expressed itself, it did so with only a portion of that wholeness. Perfection can only be achieved when the waves of the sea settle back down into the perfect stillness of being.

Until such time, enjoy the coming and going and the opportunities to either fail or succeed. Because you know perfection already at your deepest level, there is an innate pull toward home. But along the way, the waves that at times threaten to swamp you are part of the process of being-becoming-returning.

Try, if you must, to be free of flaws, and when you find yourself suffering from perceived failure or from comparing yourself to others (who are no more flawless than any other), and you have reached the point of saying, "I give up," why—this is a perfect attitude. In surrendering to the imperfection, you have acknowledged your place within wholeness.

Now perhaps as you give up the striving, you will see that you are right where you are supposed to be, who you are supposed to be, and free to simply be . . . perfect in all your imperfection.

You are so very loved.

❁ ❁ ❁

A prompt for your own experience

Enter the silence with the intention of hearing what spirit has to tell you about perfection and human flaws. Ask to know what you don't know.

Managing Disappointment

If you were a solitary actor on a stage that never changed, life would be far easier. But you are one of many beings playing your roles on an ever-changing set. Where there is interaction of this type, things do not always go as any one individual desires. This you know.

And yet when you fail to achieve your wishes, there is a feeling of letdown. Disappointment has a dimming effect that is felt. Such low vibrations trigger others of like kind, such as anger, judgment, and criticism of self and others, along with a flurry of questions.

All of these are counter to the easiest way of staying in the flow: accepting what is. Does it help to blame others? Does it help to question what went wrong and why? Yes, of course it may help avoid future disappointment to examine why things did not turn out as you wished. It may help to have the higher picture. So if you must question, then do so from the standpoint of one who wants to learn and grow.

And that, dear one, is why you are here. In awareness of the growth that occurs when you do not get your way, can you now see disappointment and setbacks as growth opportunities?

Go ahead and sulk for a while. Pouting is optional. Wallow in the fullness of your feelings and then shift to a perspective beyond the drama. Now instead of asking, "Why not?" ask instead, "Could there be a good reason I did not get my way?" In this moment's pause, you may ask for greater insights. Perhaps you will receive them and perhaps not, but one thing you can trust: Reality is what it is.

Trusting the flow, step back into it, setting aside the resistance that invariably accompanies disappointment. Once back in the flow, transmute your setback into a sense of heightened awareness.

Be on the lookout now for new outcomes, fresh opportunities that are now available to you. Disappointment is merely a waypoint along the ever-meandering river of LIFE. Do not berate or judge yourself for feeling what is very human and natural. But knowing now that you are both human and a soul, shift awareness higher and find peace.

You are so very loved.

A prompt for your own experience

Enjoy a period of meditation with the specific goal of receiving insights about dealing with disappointment. And if you hear nothing? Will you be disappointed?

Go with the flow and be curious about what unfolds.

Inner Peace

When you look at a painting, you most likely see the big picture, the gestalt. And that is the artist's intention, but a painting is made up of many strokes. If you were to focus on one small corner of a masterpiece, perhaps it would not make any sense. There would be no pattern to what you are perceiving. There is a part of your brain that is designed to create order. It is programmed to help you make choices and take actions that keep you safe. When chaos reigns, this part of the brain kicks in and takes over.

But you are more than one portion of the body. You are also a soul that is complete and whole. With awareness you can observe and begin to notice how the brain and body work together to help you deal with chaos. You can use conscious choices to breathe slowly and deeply and feel more peaceful, but these are merely Band-Aids. There is a difference between a peaceful state within the body and going within to find peace.

You will not find peace by looking within each cell or tissue or organ. Yes, it is there, for peace is the underlying, essential state of all that exists, but the distinction we are trying to make goes much deeper than within the body. The body arises from a field of consciousness that you may call the personal soul. This aspect of the soul is enacting a story. It is at this level that things can get a bit tumultuous, for stories have ups and downs. They are constantly changing.

Do keep in mind that the personal soul is part of a greater field of consciousness you may wish to call the oversoul. The oversoul is part of a group soul, and the group soul is part of a larger soul. And on and on it goes. Are you beginning to get the picture?

The field upon which you are most focused at this time—the personal soul that is living out the story of you—is immersed in many teeming fields of consciousness. These are stories upon stories. And so, you could go beyond your story and find yourself immersed in a greater story with yet another story beyond that. These are all brushstrokes making up the whole of the masterpiece. Do you see how and why life can become a bit chaotic with so much energy and information swirling about?

How then do you find the calm in the energetic chaos created by consciousness expressing itself in limitless ways? Knowing now that you cannot go beyond consciousness—for it is your very essence—you settle inward. Being holographic, each point of consciousness is a center unto itself.

Find the center of yourself and focus there. While focused on the human story, a most excellent place to place attention is the very core of you: the heart. But do not focus on the emotional heart that opens and closes dependent upon the waves of energy flowing about the field. On the contrary, go within even this center point to the point where there is no arising at all. Here you will find it, the seemingly elusive peace.

The concept of simply being may seem foreign to you. This is not being calm or being chaotic. It is the state in between these two opposites of one spectrum. Awareness swings back and forth twixt the two, but in so swinging, there is a moment's pause. This is the still point at either end.

You are already familiar at the soul level with this state of infinite stillness, but until you set the intention of coming to know it, you may pass right by it on your way from one end of the spectrum to the other.

How to find this place of complete and utter peace when the storms of the mind and the vagaries of the world threaten to push you over the edge? Step away from the edge and sink down into no-thingness. Affirm quite firmly: "I AM," with no words to follow. Do not add any story to these two words where peace resides.

I AM is the most basic state of being. All else that is added to this condition is a seed of chaos. When the swirling words and immanent imagery of life begin to draw you outward, sucking you up in the maelstrom, do not resist. Like a swimmer caught in a rip current, you will quickly tire if this is your reaction.

Instead, float, dear one. Allow yourself to be carried to the center and sink, sink, sink, knowing that instead of drowning, you will find the calm center. And in finding it, you will realize it has been here all along . . . yours for the taking. Eternally yours for the being.

You are so very loved.

A prompt for your own experience

Ask spirit to make you aware when you are getting caught up in the drama of being human. Contrast these experiences with the time you spend in expanded states of consciousness. Go there now and sink into the silence. Is there a message for you here?

Strength in Adversity

Have you seen how a child learns to walk? They hold on to something at first and pull themselves up. This introduces to them a set of muscles with which they are unfamiliar. And so, they wobble, but oh my goodness! They are standing! The world looks different from here!

They have seen those around them in such a position as this, and it feels quite powerful. And so, the child puts one foot in front of the other, still holding on, still wobbling, but there is a chortle of delight.

After a few pull-ups into what is now becoming a familiar position—this stance of standing on two feet—the child has now mastered the art of one foot in front of the other while holding on, and it is time to let go of the support.

Off they go, free from holding on . . . one step, wobble a bit, two steps, wobble a bit . . . And why are those around them pointing and expressing happy sounds so loudly? Such excitement!

And suddenly the child finds themself flat on their bum on the floor again, but the excitement is so great that they don't bother to cry. Clearly something exciting has happened here, for everyone is pointing devices at them and urging them to do it again!

And do it again they do. Pull up; hold on; then step out one, two, three; and fall. And they do this over and over, building up the strength in those wobbly legs until they are ambling like a drunken sailor from one support to the next. The tall ones continue to point devices at them and then share what is on the devices with each other. They seem quite pleased by the child's adventures at new heights.

Perhaps by now you have caught on to our analogy. Few are the humans—save those souls who chose to come into bodies incapable of walking—who have not gone through this process of learning to stand upright and ambulate on two limbs instead of four. The ability to do so was there in the vessel, latent in the muscles but undeveloped until used.

And this, dear one, is how you build resilience in other areas of your life. Strength and courage are innate aspects of the soul. They are tools you brought with you as you entered this physical vessel. You knew you would be able to call upon and use them when the challenges of life in a world of duality arose within the story. You were coached before incarnating that you might need to exercise many ancillary tools to find the strength and courage.

First and foremost among these tools, you would call out for help, just as the child does when it has fallen a bit harder than expected. It is then that the tall ones step in, for they know that taking a tumble or two is part of the growth process. But they will not let you suffer for long.

And so it is with your nonphysical helpers. They will allow you to stumble and even fall a bit, just waiting for you to reach out or call out and acknowledge that you cannot and need not do it all alone. Nor are you meant to.

Strength is within you always. Remaining aware that you are not alone and can shift awareness to the soul when in need of guidance is the practice you may wish to exercise frequently. In so doing, you no longer fear challenges. You know that you can handle any challenge before you, for you have so well practiced living lucidly as a human who knows you are also a soul.

From this awareness arises resilience. You may temporarily get knocked down, but you climb back up, ever supported from within. And is the view not far better from here?

You are so very loved.

A prompt for your own experience

Enter the silence, relax, and raise your vibration with gratitude—thanking spirit for how you have grown as a result of your earthly challenges. Radiate gratitude for the help and guidance that arise from within when you need them most. Now shift awareness beyond your human story and ask spirit to give you a message about strength and resilience.

Judgment Versus Discernment

Judging is what the human does. You are here for the full experience of LIFE, which comes in limitless varieties. No two beings are completely alike, save for the very core of each. And so, you compare. This is how you learn. This is how you remain safe. This is how you grow, by becoming aware of what is different, comparing it with past experiences of something similar, and creating meaning from the differences and the similarities.

Judgment in itself is not a good or a bad thing. It is a process. The challenge in the game of being human is when judgment is used to find only the separation instead of helping you see that which unites all. When judgment holds you locked into a certain viewpoint, there is no growth. In fact, there may be back-sliding away from evolution.

Keeping in mind the latter—moving ever onward and ever upward in your awareness that all is one—it behooves you to use discernment, which is a softer word, vibrationally, than judgment. And "To what end?" you might ask.

Well, dear one, if this story you are enacting in your human body can be likened to a game, then what would be the goal of this game? Could it be to gain as many love points as possible? If this is so, then how do you earn these points? You come in with a certain amount. Now it is up to the choices you make as to whether you lose them by actions that are not in alignment with the soul's true nature or earn more through acts of loving-kindness, compassion, service, and altruism.

Does this mean you must always be thinking of others? Not at all—you can think and act in service to the self as well. Love points thus flow.

Judgment, when used to make the self feel superior or separate, leads to losing points. Accepting that not all humans think or behave alike and sending them compassion and understanding gains points. Do you see how it works?

This is an analogy, of course. It is a way to help you understand energetically how judgment in the sense of looking down at another as inferior restricts the flow of life force. Judgment, when used to mean "discernment," does not add or detract points. It is a necessary tool for making sound decisions.

And so use your judgment to discern when you are using judgment wisely. You may ask yourself, "Am I judging this person and their behavior, or is this merely an observation?" The act of pausing to discern the difference between judging and observing racks up points.

This is not a competition, mind you, but the challenge that you as a soul willingly took on for the growth of the whole. That is the ultimate end game. And is it not a Joy to observe the flow of love in action?

You are so very loved.

A prompt for your own experience

Set aside time to truly go deep within. Shift your focus from your human story to yourself as a soul. Ask spirit to talk to you about judgment and how it shows up in your life.

Community and Fellowship

Many of you are what you would call "walking wounded." This is a term that indicates a person who is carrying trauma from previous experiences. There is not one of you who has not been affected by the words or actions of a wounded human who was not aware that all are souls and that love is all that matters.

When such is the case, hurt people hurt people. More wounds ensue, many of which are hidden under the surface. Such painful interactions can cause one to withdraw, to be suspicious of others, and to feel bitter.

"Community?" Some may scoff when hearing the word, for to them the idea of fellowship is quite distorted.

"No man is an island" is a truth worth internalizing, applying as it does to both men and women. All are deeply interconnected at the level of your true essence, the soul. Could you but see the roots that you share, you would appreciate the fellowship that is already taking place at the deeper levels. You would understand how helpful it is to break out of any self-imposed isolation and actively seek community.

You are like a grove of aspen trees, those of you who walk about in physical bodies. The roots are hidden, but they connect you as one family. Communication takes place at a subtle level that cannot be detected while you may shut yourself off at first glance.

What if you were to train yourself to look deeper and to use the eyes of the soul instead of the physical eyes? What if, when sighting another human, you brightened up at the opportunity to practice being what you came here to be: the presence of love?

"A chance to earn love points!" you might think, but how to do so? You would affirm silently, "That person is love, as am I." Yes, at first this may be a challenging exercise, but we dare say that the more you practice this, the more your commitment alone will bring to you the gift of grace: a heart opening so profound that you will realize the truth in the phrase you have been practicing.

Does this mean you will want to join a community and practice fellowship? Perhaps yes and perhaps no, but once you begin to sense the bonds that unite you, there will be a new buzz within. This pleasant sensation is one you will wish to explore further.

You will discover that it brings great pleasure to extend yourself to others simply because of the bond you now recognize between you. In so doing, you strengthen the awareness of your connectedness, and the loneliness that may have been simmering under the surface is transmuted.

And this is how it works. From wounded to healed by the salve of love. And now you are in a position to soothe the wounds of others, and you wish for as many opportunities as possible to do so. The emptiness within has been replaced by a fullness, for you are no longer experiencing separation.

Looks can be deceiving. Look upon another and remind yourself, "That is love and I AM that." In so doing, you are creating miracles.

You are so very loved.

A prompt for your own experience

Yes, ask for your own essay from spirit in meditation, *and* practice racking up love points as you interact with others throughout the day.

Overcoming Temptation

Temptations abound. Why? For the body is programmed for pleasure. You try a new food or drink or substance that alters your state to one in which you feel better and brighter, and of course you want more of this. But soon you learn a painful lesson: There can be too much of a good thing.

The body craves pleasure, but it is also programmed to tell you when enough is enough. It carries extra weight. It grows sickened by substances or activities that may temporarily feel good but that harm it in excess.

What to do when the body's proclivities ultimately bring suffering? Surrender, dear one, surrender.

"But surrender implies weakness!" you may exclaim, and we understand this. But are you not already experiencing the weakness of the will in resisting that which you know is harmful?

Hear us well: There is no blame or shame in enjoying the pleasures of life. It is the excesses that bring pain. If you wish to end suffering, do not seek to abolish pain. It is an indicator that something is out of balance. You would be better served by shifting to a surrendered state.

And herein lies the difference between weakness and strength. To surrender indicates that you no longer are willing or able to put up a fight. For humans, this implies weakness. In actuality there is great strength in observing when things have gone out of balance. There is great strength in shifting to a higher state that is no longer acting on automatic and feeding the body's impulses, and instead saying, "I am struggling to overcome these carnal desires, and enough is enough."

And so accept the way of the human body from the soul's level and be willing to say in a moment of admitting the human body's inherent weakness, "I surrender." And that is all it takes: one moment of weakness balanced with strength.

Now, dear one, you are ready to embrace the fullness of being both human and soul and enter into a new and empowered state: that of being SURRENDERED.

Feel the difference immediately in this minor change of wording. To be surrendered is to acknowledge, "I am in a human body that has little awareness compared to my higher self. I recognize the inherent power that flows through me at all times and breathes life into me here and now. I claim this power by being surrendered to it. In so doing, I experience more flow in all aspects of my life."

The paradox, dear one, is that in being surrendered, you no longer want to control. You realize that a higher consciousness can lead you to what is best for you, and you simply attune to the inner nudges about what choices to make here-now, moment by moment.

In a surrendered state, you find that temptations dissolve. Desires lessen to the point where you find new strength from within, yet it is not new at all. The inner strength that is your birthright as a soul in human form was here all along, but it was dominated by bodily forces that you in the limited human awareness allowed to pull you hither and yon.

Once you taste the joy of being surrendered to Joy, you may still seek pleasure. There is nothing wrong with this. But we dare say you will now crave and choose peace over pleasure moment by moment.

Remember this phrase: "In my surrendered state, I choose peace over pleasure," and feel the good vibrations that ensue.

Yes, of course you will still have moments of pain and pleasure. That is the way the human world is designed, but as you live a surrendered life, you will simply acknowledge the ups and downs while enjoying the higher vantage point of peace. All can exist within flow.

Peace underlies pain just as peace underlies pleasure. It is always present. When you are present in awareness as a surrendered life-form, peace is the natural choice. Nothing can tempt you, for peace is a higher vibration than temptation. Peace is of the soul, which is eternal. Lesser vibrations dissolve in the presence of peace.

Surrender once and be surrendered once and for all.

Send gratitude to this sacred body-vessel that so lovingly hosts the soul in your human experiences. It was perfectly designed to bring you to the point of "enough is enough" so that you can now experience the total peace of being surrendered to Joy.

You are so very loved.

A prompt for your own experience

Use the BLESS ME Method to enter a distinctly more expanded state of consciousness than your normal human awareness. Call on the angels and your guides to lead you in living lucidly and surrendered to higher guidance moment by moment.

Eternal Life

You speak of exploring life beyond the physical realms, and that is what you are doing in reading our words. How is it possible to tap into words and thoughts that simply arise seemingly from nowhere that make sense and convey meaning? It is possible for there is a limitless, infinite field of being from which all beings arise.

Think about your dreams at night. Where do you go? The body does not leave the bed, yet you are having adventures in seemingly far-off places. And what if the body is part of its own dreamlike reality? "But it is quite real!" you protest, for the body is right here when you awaken from your nighttime dreams.

Yes, but what is the body? It is a collection of sensations, thoughts, and images. Think about it: You know the body because you can see it and feel it and believe in it. But are not all these simply experiences in awareness? And where does this awareness reside? Why, the same place in which your dreams reside: not in the head, but in the mind, which is the same mind from which all states arise.

Could it be that your body and all other experiences arise within the one mind of God? Could this mind be the infinite field from which all thoughts and dreams arise? Yes, they are one and the same.

And this field . . . do you think it ever goes away?

It seems to go away, dear one, when you think. We have asked you twice so far to think about something, and in so doing you revert to patterns based on past experience. Now see what happens when we ask you not to think but to simply be here now.

To do so requires you to set all thoughts, sensations, and feelings aside. In other words, to be without experience, which is the activity of the mind. Do you see? When the mind is still, you touch eternity.

Stories come and go, for experiences come and go. Lives come and go, for what is a life but a series of experiences of identifiable life-forms. And in between the coming and going is a pause. This is akin to the waves of the ocean settling down to stillness. The waves may appear to have gone away, but they have simply reverted to their natural state as inseparable expressions or "arisings" of the ocean. They do not go away, nor do you, dear one, when the physical dream ends.

Oh, we hear you protest calling this experience in a body a dream, but what is a dream? An experience within a state of consciousness that has certain characteristics. This is life, and you are eternally part of it.

Life is like the ocean. It is eternally here. Life in physical form is one expression—one arising—of life. You, as a wave within the ocean, are either rising up or settling down. The ocean exists for all eternity.

You derive your very being from this state of being that knows and has no end. Your source arises to create worlds upon worlds . . . from a world or state of being with no end. Explore your true and eternal nature by being willing to set the story of you aside.

Explore the silence and discover how the mind works. Watch and experience how it rises up and settles down, rises up, and settles down. And while you are exploring, should you encounter other waves—other minds—why, engage them! Dance and play until you both settle back down to the same state of being.

Explore, experience, engage. In this way you will come to know eternity without having to think about it.

You are so very loved.

A prompt for your own experience

Have you been sitting in peace daily? The SIP of the Divine is an easy way to explore the nature of the mind and to experience "being" in between the sensations, thoughts, and feelings that arise and subside eternally. Sit in peace and ask spirit to talk to you about eternal life.

Solitude and Reflection

Do you know those who must surround themselves with distractions? There is always noise, perhaps to drown out the noise inside the head. And that noise is generally not quite supportive of who they really are. Do you recognize this behavior?

There is a voice inside that chatters incessantly. And what if it is trying to get your attention?

"But I don't want to hear what it is trying to tell me," you may protest, and we understand this. The inner voice of your human self can be quite biting and cruel. But if you were to dig a bit deeper, what you might hear are the voices of long buried emotions crying, "Let us out!"

And therein lies the challenge. Until and unless you are willing to allow to arise what is buried deep within, you cannot hear the deepest voice that underlies all the clatter and clamoring.

Perhaps you were wounded by another lashing out in an attempt to avoid the noise within themselves. Do you see how pain is passed down?

What to do? Pay attention to the pain. It is an indicator that something is out of balance. How will sitting in the silence help? Once you realize you are not the pain, but a higher being who has existed for all eternity beyond the story in which the pain arises, now you can take on a higher perspective.

Observe what is churning and burning inside. Can you mother it? Can you lovingly coax it out and say, "There, there, I know you are seeking attention. I hear you. I appreciate your desire to be noticed. I am here for you. What do you wish to tell me?"

You may well observe that once noticed and heard, all that clamor goes into a state of shock. "We are being listened to!" And now all bets are off.

Once you are willing to sit in solitude and listen to what the voices within have been trying to tell you, they will settle down. No, it is not the same as when they go back into hiding. They are simply feeling loved for the first time. "We have been noticed. We are valued. Perhaps now we need not create such havoc."

All anyone or any thought form ever wants is to be heard, appreciated, and loved, dear one. It is why our words to you feel so good. We hear you. You are in pain. You would rather avoid the pain, but running away is only avoidance. Do not run from the darkness. Bring in what is missing: the light, the light, the light.

And where does that light come from? The soul, and you are that!

Turn up the inner light that has been blocked by so much avoidance, so much shoving down of the pain. Shine that deep, inner light onto the pain and sit with it. Comfort it. Nurture it. "There, there . . . I understand where you are coming from. I was not there for you in the past by being present, but I am here now, ready to listen and set you free. You need not act out as you have in the past. We can release your angst as you tell me how you would like to serve the whole of us now."

Do you see? In sitting in solitude with curiosity, you discover that there is truly nothing to fear, for what you feel you can heal . . . through loving-kindness to what is.

Reflect on this in solitude, why don't you? Insights will flow like water once you ask to see what has led to the chaos within and how to heal it all with love.

Quiet moments are not the enemy. They are your salvation. Embrace solitude. Reflect on the beautiful wholeness of you as a soul in human form, and we dare say you will begin to see the love that you are reflected all around you.

You are so very loved.

❁ ❁ ❁

A prompt for your own experience

Sit in silence and ask to be shown what you have buried deep within. Listen with curiosity from a higher place. Be the source of comfort and love to whatever arises. Write any insights that arise from the spirit within.

Service and Philanthropy

Money is valuable far beyond the meaning that you give it. You see coins and bills and read the numbers on their faces and think this is what they are worth. But oh, the growth that can be had by seeing money not as something that must be amassed in large quantities in order to be happy, but as a means of understanding flow.

The human brain is programmed for survival. It gives you the sense of "never enough." This is ego, dear one. Notice this programming. Acknowledge it, and then shift to the soul's perspective, where there is the awareness that what is needed is always provided.

In a world that is ever-changing, flow is the key. To worry about money and trying to amass more and more of it leaves one in an imbalanced state in which one only focuses upon what is coming in and parses what is going out. This is not flow. This is stagnation and imbalance.

We are not saying that your expenses must equal your income to achieve balance. We are recommending that you try giving your gifts of not just money but service to others and see how this changes things.

When you no longer fear "not enough" and give from the heart, heart energy flows back to you. When you are self-absorbed, you lose sight of what matters most: your interconnectedness.

If you are feeling lonely, observe the results when you get out of your isolation by helping others. Suddenly you feel a lift, for you have activated the soul connection that is always present.

Stinginess and generosity are two sides of one coin. We are not suggesting that you give until it hurts. As in all things, find the balance. Play with this spectrum of attachment and letting go. Where is the sweet spot?

We return to our initial discussion of money as a tool. It is a necessity in your world, but it also has much to teach you. As you hold on to what you have earned and experience fear of losing it, life in general does not flow as freely as it will when you remember that what you give out comes back to you.

Do you see now the connection between money and generosity of self? We say again: What you give out comes back to you, perhaps not in kind, but in ways unimagined when you cling tightly to what you think is yours.

In a world where all is interconnected, concepts of "mine" and "yours" are artifacts. They are necessary, to be sure, but they can hold you prisoner to greed and fear until and unless you see them as the keys to finding freedom. "What's mine is yours" will set you free.

Give freely of yourself. Philanthropy comes in many forms. If you don't know where to begin, go within, why don't you. As in all things, spirit will guide your every move.

You are so very loved.

A prompt for your own experience

Enter an expanded state of consciousness and ask spirit to show you a new way in which you can share your highest self and make a difference in the world. Intend to receive insights beyond what you might have imagined.

Marriage and Relationships

What is love? It is the recognition that there is no separation between you and another. You say you fall in love, but you simply remember a deeper truth that never leaves you.

If you were not meant to be in relationship with others, you would feel no attraction, but the pull to share your life with another is a natural urge. It exists, many believe, for the continuation of the species. This is true, but marriage and other relationships also exist for the growth opportunities such entanglements provide.

"Entanglements?" you say, as you hear what feels to you like an unusual word to use in relation to something that seems quite sacred. Indeed, marriage is sacred, for two become one unit, and in your scientific terms, this is precisely what entanglement refers to. Your energy fields are so interrelated that you begin to know each other's thoughts, and you act in unison, many times without thinking.

At first the other half of this singular unit you call a relationship can do no wrong. This is the human version of love. It occurs because their presence and their adoration of you allows you to feel special and appreciated. You do the same for the apparent other. But after a while, when the newness of human love wears off, the relationship becomes less about "us" and more about "What's in it for me, me, me?"

This is when the true opportunities for growth arise. Relationships—if they are to remain healthy—require an ongoing dance from me, to you, to us. They require one to listen, truly hear, and understand another at a level beneath the surface. When there is an imbalance of these requirements, suffering ensues.

We have often said that those who push your buttons are your greatest teachers, and most often these teachers are the ones you live with. In many cases, after the initial onslaught of human desire, your human nature will cause you to find fault with the apparent other and wish to change them to align with your way of seeing and being.

In fact, relationship challenges are your greatest opportunity to learn that life is not about changing anything that appears outside yourself. It is about coming to align with the one self within by allowing LIFE to flow. It is about making choices that bring you into that flow. If you are struggling and butting heads with another, you have stopped flowing.

In a marriage, you make a vow to stay together until death do you part. And yet through these conversations, perhaps you are learning that death is not the end. Those with whom you are in relationship are members of a soul family. You travel through many lifetimes together, often changing roles from one incarnation to the next. Death does not part you. You will continue learning and flowing together through the will of God. Relationships are the way you do so.

Make your vows, but do not stay in a relationship that is abusive. Even the painful aspects of entanglement serve a purpose. They allow you to choose self-respect and self-love. You may work things out at this level or a higher one until in the end, all remember that the purpose of life is to shine brightly and be the presence of love.

Must you be in a relationship to learn and grow? No. There will come fallow periods when self-reflection and solitude lead to growth. But ultimately you as source created many selves for the joy of entanglement. Seek friendships. Seek a partner. Enjoy the dance of relating to others for the fullness of LIFE.

You are so very loved.

A prompt for your own experience

Use the BLESS ME Method to enter a meditative state and ask spirit to show you what you have learned from the most important relationships in your life. Ask to be shown how you have grown as a result. Ask for any relationship advice that will help you in your journey here and now.

Guides and Angels

There are many misconceptions about your unseen helpers in the higher realms. Throughout the ages, angels have been depicted with wings. Yes, this is how they may appear to some so that they can be recognized, but they need not take form at all. They are light beings of the highest caliber, able to leap tall buildings and even pass through said buildings to bring you aid and succor.

Does this sound like a fantasy? Are they truly superheroes? What is a superhero? One who has abilities beyond the normal human and who can effect miracles. So yes, angels are superheroes.

There is a reason you revere them, but it is not just for their abilities to bring assistance and relief. They bring you far more than that, dear one. They bring you love. So much of your suffering would lessen if you knew you were loved beyond words. And oh, yes, you are so very loved.

You cannot see us, your guides and angels, so it is up to you to move beyond the necessity to see the help that comes your way, to feel us physically, or to hear our words through human ears. We are here playing our part in your journey of awakening, which begins with belief.

Children love and often believe fairy tales. There is a reason for this. The stories of magical figures rendering assistance when needed take them back to the knowing they brought with them into this world.

You were a child once. Your body may have aged, and you may have experienced human trials and traumas that no longer allow you to believe in fairy tales, but the feeling of magic and wonder and the desire for such has never gone away.

Find that feeling again. It exists because angels and guides are very real. This magical connection remains alive within you for a reason: to take you back to your real home, which is not some far-off place but a knowing within you . . . the awareness that you are never alone. You are part of creation itself, which connects all that is through the fibers of love.

Call on the angels to make their presence known to you. Thank them even when you cannot sense them. Reignite your friendship with the guides and inspirers who know you better than you know yourself. Talk to them frequently and feel the stirring in your heart. Angels are real!

Guides keep you on track for the purposes you came into a body—your soul's plan. Those gentle nudges you call intuition? They are in many cases your guides and angels doing their part. Act on those nudges when they are helpful and see how life flows as you do so. Come to trust in the subtle guidance, and you may well find the guidance is no longer subtle but loud and clear.

Synchronicities become the norm as you open to the presence of nonphysical assistance at every twist and turn. Feathers fall on your path from no observed source . . . could it be from an angel's wing? "But you said you don't have wings!" we hear you exclaim, and we say that anything is possible when you open to the world of possibilities from which you and all of us arise.

It is a wondrous world, indeed. Won't you join us in celebrating presence?

You are so very loved.

A prompt for your own experience

If you are not already in the habit of calling on your guides and angels (can you say, "Hey, Spirit!"), begin now to talk with them regularly. Shift awareness to the heart, and ask to establish a more conscious connection with them throughout the day. Whether you sense them or not, send gratitude for their presence and loving assistance.

Dealing with Change

What is grace? A gift of ease . . . those moments when you do not have to try to achieve something—it simply happens. You do nothing alone. You may think you do, but what of the trillions of cells in your body? Do you take credit for those? It is by grace that you exist in a body with trillions of cells that know exactly how to maintain balance.

And what does this have to do with the topic at hand, with change? Why, everything. The cells in your body are not the same ones you were born with. They change often. They come into existence and they die . . . just as do all things in LIFE . . . including the entirety of the body, while you, the soul, continue on by grace.

The body provides the vehicle for you to experience LIFE. And what is life but a process of ever-changing experiences. And what are experiences but patterns of sensations, thoughts, and feelings arising and subsiding in awareness. Nothing is permanent, save the awareness from which the experiences arise.

If you are to understand change and navigate transitions between experiences better, then see awareness as the ocean and all else as waves. See the cycles of coming and going, rising and subsiding, as quite natural.

With this awareness, perhaps you will no longer resist the waves. When you resist what is present in awareness, you stiffen and become rigid. With rigidity you suffer. The solution is to do what one does in a rip current: cease resisting and flow. Now you do not run the risk of tiring yourself out and drowning. Instead you rise when the waves rise and go down into the troughs when they subside. You do not panic, for you know they will go up again, by grace.

Change is uncomfortable, for it brings with it new wave patterns. You can feel these undulations in your energy field. The brain often reacts to change with fear until you determine what is needed to be safe.

Once again, when you resist what is—be it the sudden lack of patterns you have enjoyed for many cycles when one you love crosses the veil or new patterns you have not yet experienced as the result of any change—you risk being swamped by the waves. Step onto the life raft of awareness and ride out the undulations.

There will be times when you lack the strength to take action as change occurs. Float.

There will be times when you feel you cannot go on. Call out "Hey, Spirit!" and ask for assistance.

There will be times when you notice you are actually enjoying the newness that change brings. Like an artist with a fresh canvas, dip into your palette and see what new patterns you can create.

This is LIFE in all its fullness, dear one. Change is simply the result of the ongoing flow of the creator's brush.

You are so very loved.

A prompt for your own experience

Enter a meditative state. Truly take the time to settle in and become as still as possible. Ask spirit to give you insights about how you deal with change. Are there patterns of resistance that spirit may help you transmute into greater flow? Listen and learn.

Dealing with Regret

There will always be moments you wish you could do over. Why is this? For humans learn by trial and error.

And so you will err. You will make choices that result in less than positive outcomes. This causes a feeling within you that you know as regret, but let us examine this feeling without giving it a label. As you may know by now, feelings are simply indicators. They are gifts that compel you to take action.

This gift you call regret is a feeling that says, in effect, "I do not care for this outcome. If I had chosen differently or acted differently, the situation now would be better than it is." And better, dear one, is the evolutionary goal of each choice. An artist puts dabs of paint here and there not to make the painting worse but to improve it. Why else paint at all?

And so, as you create your current masterpiece that you call your life, there will be strokes of paint that did not come out the way you intended. "Yes, and the painting is ruined!" you cry. "There is no fixing it!" Perhaps this is so with the current painting, but you remain the eternal artist.

Each work of art has something to teach you. Each brushstroke leads to another with greater mastery. To ruminate on past strokes that did not come out as you intended is indeed to remain stuck in place with your creativity stagnating.

You came here to create and evolve. Regret is merely an indicator that there is a better brushstroke to be had. If you cannot mend what was created with your misplaced brushstroke, perhaps you need a fresh canvas.

The previous one will remain forever in awareness, but see it as it is: an experience that led you to fresh opportunities. Make your amends as you are guided and then return to the present moment to paint again. That is how life flows. Regret is fuel. It ensures you do not go around creating mindlessly. See it in this way and vow to move forward expressing your potential as you are designed by the great creator to do.

You are so very loved.

A prompt for your own experience

Choose an event in your life that you wish had turned out differently. Take it into meditation and ask spirit to help you see it in a w-holy new light. What insights can you gain based on the words above and how higher consciousness makes the issue personal to you?

Balancing Humility and Confidence

Where does confidence come from? It arises when you know that you can accomplish what you desire. You trust that you will not be impeded in reaching your goal. Confidence can come with cockiness or humility. This is how to know if you are aligned with your restricted human aspect or with the soul.

The soul knows no bravado. It knows only the utter humility of being the light. With this knowing comes an unshakable faith that all is well, no matter what. With this surrendering to a higher power beyond the self, which is the genesis of humility, comes the gratitude that maintains in awareness a state of connection to all that is.

Without this awareness, it is all too easy for the human to slip back into a false state of "I can do it myself." Be on the lookout for such an attitude and watch out when you notice it. This type of confidence can lead to a fall you would do well to avoid.

But then, humans learn from pain, do they not?

If you wish your lessons to be as painless as possible, you are well-advised to notice when ego rears its head, acknowledge it, and set it aside. In so doing, you bow with humility to the father and mother of all creation . . . the headmasters of this school that is not some sort of punishment but a stage on which you in your human role get to practice your creative gifts.

The lessons of life come through trial and error. You will fall down and get back up again, for the soul knows you are here to learn and grow. May it humble you to know you chose every bit of it: the pain and the pleasure, the wows and the boredom, the friends and the foes, for the joy that would emerge as you learn to step off the stage and enter the silence in the wings.

There, held in the arms of love, you can still—in every moment—be reminded. There, in the stillness, you remember once again your innate and true power as the light of consciousness.

Do you see how there is power in humility? From this place of knowing "I am the Light" is born a confidence free of pride. This is a state imbued with gratitude. It carries you forward, knowing you can remain confident yet humbled as you declare, "Thy will be done!"

This is the balanced state that will ensure peace and joy in all things: humility balanced with confidence, surrender balanced with action, soul balanced with your human role. Maintaining such a state is quite simple when you remain awake and aware of who you really are.

You are so very loved. It can be no other way, beautiful light.

A prompt for your own experience

Set aside the time to spend at least 10 minutes quieting the busy mind by focusing on the breath. Move awareness to the heart as you breathe slowly, deeply, and rhythmically. Once in a peaceful, expanded state of consciousness, affirm that you are always connected to a source of wisdom that will guide you in all things. In this state, ask that your human lessons be as painless as possible. Ask for insights about confidence and humility. As you receive them, engage the source of the words you hear for any further guidance that will help you in your earthly journey.

Self-Worth and Acceptance

Whoever told you that you are not worthy? You need not have heard these words to take them on as part of your belief system. You see, the brain is programmed to compare and contrast. In so doing, you form ideas of better and worse, worthy and unworthy. The more attention you give to any concept, the more it grows.

You live in a world where physical beauty is prized, and you compare your appearance with others'. Your world values the amassing of money and material goods, and you thus compare your possessions with others'. Human beings value titles and accomplishments, and you thus compare yourself with the perceived successes of others.

Tune in now and feel how the body reacts as you read and think about concepts such as beauty, wealth, and success. Do you feel in any way diminished? Hear us now: These are human concepts born of your cultural upbringing. What if you lived in a community where money was not a factor, where all looked alike? Why then, some other factor of comparison, such as physical strength, would come into play, for that is, once again, the human way.

How to overcome thoughts of unworthiness? Acknowledge that you are not only human, dear soul. You know this deep inside, which is why an aspect of you rebels when your ego tries to tell you that you do not live up to a constructed human standard.

The light within you shines eternally. Yes, at times one light may shine more brightly than another, but as the light of consciousness, there is no comparing you with other lights. Light is light. All exist to shine the light of God upon the world and to know, "It is G(o)od."

Can you accept that you are unique? Of course. This is quite obvious. Now tell the brain that you are grateful it is doing its job to seek out danger and cast it away, but that its tendency to compare your beautiful self with others is not helping you shine your light.

Accept that the brain will try to tell you that you do not live up to some human standards and that you may exceed others' ideals. This is the way of the brain, but you are far more than a mass of human tissue, blood, and bones. Go beyond the physical heart to the very core of you. There you will discover that which is identical in every creation: the spiritual heart.

There is no comparison with this heart of hearts. There is no better or worse. There is only being. Find this place in you and know your intrinsic worth. Know your inestimable value. Know that the truest you has nothing to do with a story filled with success and failure, judgment and acceptance.

In recognizing your true nature, acceptance of the story comes naturally. If you struggle to find self-worth and acceptance, cease seeking within the confines of your human story. Go deeper. Go silent. Go to the core. There you are. Neither worthy nor unworthy, but the purest of pure . . . light.

And that, dear one, is worth knowing.

You are so very loved.

A prompt for your own experience

Enter a meditative state and ask to be shown where you judge yourself harshly. Request that spirit inspire with words to let you truly believe you are worthy of all blessings and loved without condition.

The Power of Surrender

What does it mean to "just be"? This is a state in which there is no trying or striving. It is a condition of flow in which you know you are guided moment by moment. As you surrender to this flow, you notice that all tasks become easier. You become aware that each step is lighter. There is an ease unknown to most humans.

Why do more not know this way of being? For they have not found the still point at the center. They are still swirling about in thought patterns going round and round. These patterns carry distracting advice and convey falsehoods that hold the human in bondage to ideas of "must, have to, need to, and should."

In the surrendered state, there are none of these obligations. Yes, there are still tasks that require your human efforts, but in the surrendered state, you go about them knowing you are being guided.

How do you come to know this? You step out, and then you pause and listen. Take action based on what you hear, sense, or simply know. Then step out again, pause, and act on what you again know is the next step and the next step and the next one, for they arise with clarity from within.

Is this weakness to act in this way, pausing to discern the best next step or action? Not at all, dear one. There is great strength in acknowledging you are part of a greater whole that wishes only for you to join in and serve.

There is a reason human beings join groups. Great satisfaction comes from serving something bigger than the smaller self. Yes, you take care of the self as necessary, but in working as part of a team or family you find the state of connection that the soul knows quite well.

You are all light beings temporarily in human form. As light, you cannot be divided. As bodies, you stand apart. How to reconcile this duality? Integrate your awareness of being both human and spirit by surrendering to the power of higher consciousness.

Yes, you are wise. Yes, you are strong. Yes, you could do it yourself, and we ask you, how has that worked for you in the past? At times it has served you quite well to act as the sovereign human you are, and you achieved what you desired. And then? When that achievement's sparkle wore off, then what? Was there not another and another and another must-have, must-do, must-win prize? How very tiring!

We are not saying that in surrendering you give up the gold or the glitter. We are telling you that these will flow quite naturally as you allow yourself to be guided in every moment. Step, pause, listen, act. It is a simple formula for peace.

What is most important is understanding precisely what it is you are pausing to listen to. The soul knows. The soul knows that in the silence, you tap into guidance, and knowing that will lead to the next step.

That next step is not always known until the present moment unfolds, for there are so many other souls stepping out at the same time. If you fail to surrender, you may step on toes and trip repeatedly. If you pause before the next step, the freshest, most helpful guidance will bubble up based on what is known from within the web at a now-level yet unseen or heard by human ears.

Step, pause, listen, act, why don't you? The surrendering takes place in the willingness to follow this simple pattern, knowing you are serving not only the self but the greater good. This is integration within duality: seeing self and others as one dancing wholeness.

There is great power in surrendering to the higher power of the web. You need not know from which level the guidance comes at any one moment. Set the intention to be consciously connected and divinely guided by source at whatever level serves best in each moment, and you will find that state of flow and ease.

By grace it is so.

You are so very loved.

A prompt for your own experience

Are you ready to surrender to source? Step, pause, listen, and act.

Step now to a quiet place and pause long enough to go deeply within. Listen to whatever spirit has to share with you right here, right now. Listen with trust from the heart until you hear words that you know without doubt are your next step on this wondrous journey you're on. Come back then to waking consciousness and act, giving gratitude as you do so for the gifts spirit eternally puts in your path.

AFTERWORD

Now You're Listening

There is a reason that surrender is the theme of the final essay in Part II. Surrender goes hand in hand with trust when you acknowledge that you are part of a much greater reality and live accordingly. As my guides, Sanaya, advised in one of their daily messages:

> *Be surrendered. This is a most powerful state. You need only say once, "Enough is enough. I am tired of struggling. I am tired of trying to do it all myself. I wish to be led and supported by a higher power, for what I have been doing and how I have been living is too hard. I surrender."*
>
> *There, perhaps you may call that weakness. We call that coming home. Now you can live in a powerful, ongoing surrendered state in which the guidance and companionship you seek is ever-present in awareness. Be surrendered and thrive.*

Do you relinquish control when you surrender to source? Not at all. You allow that there is a higher power that flows through and manifests as all things, including you. You recognize that you can control some things, but not all. This is the challenging part for the ego, which likes to think that it is always in control, but clinging tightly to the need for things to go your way brings frustration, restriction, and suffering.

It is my sincere desire that having read this book and done the practices, you will establish a highly personal and intimate connection with spirit. When you live surrendered and turn to spirit first for guidance and insights, you put ego in its rightful place as a helpful tool for carrying out the soul's intentions.

It has been a pleasure and an honor to include in this book stories and mention of my assistants, Patty, Stephanie, Christy, Bev, Meredith, and Jayesh. I end this book by bringing in another valued member of my team, Melissa Knutson. She and the story that follows provide a fitting final example of the practical assistance—not to mention the joy and wonder—that result when you live a consciously connected and divinely guided life.*

Soon after I hired Melissa as my "correspondence curator," the hot spot she had been using to connect to the Internet died. She realized that she needed a better source of Wi-Fi for her new duties and ordered a high-tech router.

Two days later she received a notification on her phone that the router had been delivered. When she saw the photo of the spot where the courier had left her pricey purchase, Melissa groaned. Packages were supposed to be left in a

---

* You can learn more about this path to awakened living and enjoy a collection of helpful tools and techniques in my Hay House book *The Awakened Way*.

parcel collection area, but the photo clearly showed the box propped against a door that Melissa didn't recognize.

Her first thought was, *I'm in trouble.*

Melissa lives in a very large apartment complex with numerous multifamily buildings. The photo revealed only the bottom of a nondescript door with no identifying numbers.

She headed directly for the office on the far side of the massive complex. Once she located a staff person, she described her plight. With a sense of urgency, she explained that she needed the router for an upcoming meeting. The receptionist listened with sympathy but shrugged helplessly. No one had brought in an errant package, and there was no way of tracking it.

Frustrated and fighting panic, Melissa stepped outside into the sunshine. Intuitive and empathic for most of her life, she acknowledged her emotional discomfort and paused to take a deep breath. Instantly centered, she closed her eyes and acknowledged her abiding faith and trust in an ever-present source.

Spirit, she said silently, *I believe this job with Suzanne is a divine appointment. I want you to prove it to me by miraculously helping me find this package easily and immediately.*

When she opened her eyes, she began walking straight ahead toward a set of tan colored buildings. After only a few steps, she heard the words, *Turn left.*

Melissa glanced to the left and saw several light-yellow buildings. She paused long enough to pull out her phone and study the photo of the box's location. The walls around the door where the package was propped appeared more tan than yellow. She began to continue her path toward the tan buildings and heard, *No. Turn left.*

Okay, fine, Melissa said silently, trusting and surrendering to the voice within.

She turned left as guided and walked past a shrubby area toward the nearest set of apartments. Glancing down when she reached the first building, she stared in disbelief. There, semi-hidden and tucked down a set of stairs, sat her package.

Melissa later recounted this story on my *Awakened Way* podcast and shared her reaction with the audience. "It really was miraculous!" she exclaimed. "It's a huge complex. You have no idea how long it would have taken me to find it," she said, adding, "I saw that as validation that everything really is aligned."

Yes, Melissa. You're right. It really is.

Despite the often-chaotic events we read about and sometimes experience in our human lives, there is an underlying order. When you come into alignment with the soul and shift to its higher perspective from a state of wholeness, miracles and synchronicities become the norm.

I began this book by contrasting our modern habit of relying on technology with the practice of listening to the spirit within when we need comfort or direction. I end it with this example of a dear friend and colleague instinctively using her inner guidance to locate her modern tech gear!

Such an instinctive action can occur for you as well when you make a commitment to regularly turn within, ask for assistance, and listen for spirit's reply.

The external world will constantly pull you in multiple directions. Trust that you are always connected to source in the many ways it manifests and live surrendered. Find the still center from which *divine* direction arises, and spirit will speak.

Bravo, beautiful soul. Now you're listening.

ACKNOWLEDGMENTS

This book, like anything that we create in this world, could not have come about without a team effort.

First and always, my deepest gratitude goes to the love of my life, my soulmate and husband, Ty. Thank you for never begrudging the scratching pen noises at three in the morning or the hours I spend at my computer when a wave of inspiration insists on flowing. Your love, patience, humor, and never-ending support make it possible for me to say, "Aye, aye!" when Spirit says, *"Now hear this."*

I am profoundly grateful for my wonderful assistants, past and present, whose enthusiasm, commitment, and heart-centered service allow The Awakened Way teachings to reach people around the globe. What I do would not be possible without your skill, care, and tireless support behind the scenes. The love we share for each other is a unique blessing that I wish all work teams could enjoy. It would change our world as you have enriched mine.

My heartfelt thanks go to my editor, Sally Mason-Swaab, and to everyone at Hay House, including Amy Kiberd—the first to champion my work. You all expertly helped transform what began as an idea scribbled on the back of a napkin (thank you, Patty Gift!) into a book with the potential to touch hearts, open minds, and change lives. I truly appreciate and honor your belief in this work, your professionalism, and your shared commitment to uplifting humanity.

And finally, my eternal gratitude to Joy—the voice, the presence, the knowing behind these words. Thank you for the conversations, the guidance, the love, and the reminders that we are all expressing you with every breath. To understand and celebrate the paradox of being Joy-us is a blessing beyond words.

ABOUT THE AUTHOR

Spiritual teacher and medium **Suzanne Giesemann** knows how to live in a left-brained world. As a Navy commander and aide to the head of the U.S. military on 9/11, she was unaware of anything beyond this earthly realm. The death of her pregnant stepdaughter by lightning strike catapulted Suzanne on a journey that led to the unexpected gift of evidence-based communication with nonphysical consciousness.

Known for her joyful, down-to-earth style and making deep spiritual concepts easy to understand, Suzanne laces her teaching with evidence-filled stories of the greater reality and practical tools that provide proof of our multidimensional nature.

She has authored numerous books, six best-selling Hemi-Sync recordings, and YouTube videos reaching millions of viewers. She produces the Awakened Way app with daily inspirational messages and hosts the top-ranking *Awakened Way* podcast. She leads classes, workshops, and retreats in person and online to help people make the shift to a divinely guided life.

Website: **suzannegiesemann.com**

Hay House Titles of Related Interest

YOU CAN HEAL YOUR LIFE, the movie,
starring Louise Hay & Friends
(available as an online streaming video)
www.hayhouse.com/louise-movie

THE SHIFT, the movie,
starring Dr. Wayne W. Dyer
(available as an online streaming video)
www.hayhouse.com/the-shift-movie

A BEGINNER'S GUIDE TO THE UNIVERSE: Uncommon Ideas for Living an Unusually Happy Life, by Mike Dooley

INFINITE LIFE, INFINITE LESSONS: Wisdom from the Spirit World on Living, Dying, and the In-Between, by Susan Grau

READ LIFE ACCURATELY: Recognize and Respond to What's Really Happening, by Sonia Choquette

YOU ARE A CHANNEL: Receive Guidance from Higher Realms, Ascended Masters, Star Families, and More, by Sara Landon

All of the above are available at your local bookstore,
or may be ordered by contacting Hay House (see next page).

We hope you enjoyed this Hay House book. If you'd like to receive our online catalog featuring additional information on Hay House books and products, or if you'd like to find out more about the Hay Foundation, please contact:

Hay House LLC, P.O. Box 5100, Carlsbad, CA 92018-5100
(760) 431-7695 or (800) 654-5126
www.hayhouse.com® • www.hayfoundation.org

Published in Australia by:
Hay House Australia Publishing Pty Ltd
18/36 Ralph St., Alexandria NSW 2015
Phone: +61 (02) 9669 4299
www.hayhouse.com.au

Published in the United Kingdom by:
Hay House UK Ltd
The Sixth Floor, Watson House,
54 Baker Street, London W1U 7BU
Phone: +44 (0) 203 927 7290
www.hayhouse.co.uk

Published in India by:
Hay House Publishers (India) Pvt Ltd
Muskaan Complex, Plot No. 3,
B-2, Vasant Kunj, New Delhi 110 070
Phone: +91 11 41761620
www.hayhouse.co.in

HAY
HOUSE